THREE STUDIES IN
SIMPLICITY

THREE STUDIES IN SIMPLICITY

—:—   —:—   —:—

PADRE PIO

MARTIN DE PORRES

BENEDICT THE BLACK

—:—   —:—   —:—

By
MALACHY CARROLL
and
POL DE LEON ALBARET O.F.M.

FRANCISCAN HERALD PRESS
Chicago, Illinois 60609

Three Studies in Simplicity: Padre Pio, Martin de Porres, Benedict the Black, the first two authored by, the last translated by Malachy Carroll from the French of Pol de Leon Albaret's *Sainte Benedict l'Africaine*, Editions Franciscaines, Paris, France, 1960. Copyright © 1974 by Franciscan Herald Press, 1434 West 51st Street, Chicago, Illinois 60609.

Library of Congress Cataloging in Publication Data:

Main entry under title

Three studies in simplicity.

     CONTENTS: Carroll, M. Padre Pio. — Carroll, M. Martin de Porres. — Albaret, Pol de Léon. Benedict the Black.

     1. Pio da Pietrelcina, Father.   2. Martin de Porres, Saint, 1579-1639.   3. Benedetto da San Filadelfo, Saint, 1526-1589. I. Carroll, Malachy Gerard, 1918-   Padre Pio. 1974. II. Carroll, Malachy Gerard, 1918-   St. Martin de Porres. 1974.
III. Albaret, Pol de Léon, Father, 1906-   Benedict l'Africain. English.
BX4655.2.T45   282′.092′2 [B]   74-8284

ISBN 0-8199-0533-X

Made in the United States of America.

~~~~~~

NIHIL OBSTAT:
  Mark Hegener O.F.M.
  Censor Deputatus

IMPRIMATUR:
  Msgr. Richard A. Rosemeyer, J.C.D.
  Vicar General, Archdiocese of Chicago

March 25, 1974
Chicago, Illinois

CONTENTS

I. PADRE PIO

v

II. MARTIN DE PORRES

III. BENEDICT THE BLACK

I

PADRE PIO

1. PRELUDE TO THE STORY

There are two words which suggest to the man in the street, balloons in mid-air, attached to nothing and filled with "airy nothing." They are the words *metaphysics* and *mysticism*. As to the first, he has the general impression that it is the scientific term for muddling yourself methodically. As to mysticism, he applauds the pun that equates it often with "misty schism"; or if he meets its physical manifestation in the form of ecstasies, levitation, stigmata, telekinesis, or in any other form, he either takes up a mule-like stance of stupified unbelief, or he rushes forward with wild uncritical enthusiasm, his mouth wide open to swallow all.

A word like *stigmata* is very evocative. It means that the wounds of Christ are traced in some fashion on the human body. The supreme example of this is St. Francis of Assisi, who catches the imagination of men because he was so Christ-like, and because in him humility and meekness walked again in the world's ways, bearing the wounds of Christ. The enthusiasm of Br. Elias, in his letter to the minister provincial in France, has been echoed in every century: "I announce to you great joy, even a new miracle. . . ."

There can be no doubt concerning the authenticity of St. Francis' stigmata; but in a book which deals with a stigmatic of the twentieth century, it is imperative to sound in advance the note

3

of prudence and of caution. A word can suggest a world; and the world which the word "stigmatization" suggests is a world in which the wounds of Christ may certainly have been laid burningly in the bodies of certain chosen ones, but which is certainly also a world of deliberate fakes and mountebanks. The word *caveat* is here written large.

As early as 1222, prior to the receiving of the stigmata by St. Francis, we find Matthew Paris recording the case of a man who was "deluded" — *obcaecatus* — into the belief that he bore the wounds of Christ. Later in the same century, we find another recording the imprisonment of "a certain rustic who used to crucify himself." This was apparently linked with the obsession that he was the Son of God and the redeemer of the world.

Three centuries later came the notorious cases of Magdalena de la Cruz and Maria de la Visitación. A halo of renown surrounded the name of Abbess Magdalena of Cordova, and homage was paid to her even by the Empress Isabella, until, frightened by sickness, Magdalena confessed to years of fraud. The Portuguese Dominican nun, Sor Maria de la Visitación was even more renowned. At the time when the Armada was being prepared to sail against England, this nun of Lisbon exercised quite an astounding influence. Before her downfall, her name figures in state dispatches and even in commander's reports. Father Thurston (*The Physical Phenomena of Mysticism,* p. 88), in a fascinating account of Sor Maria, suggests that "very possibly the fact that the five wounds were figured in the arms of Portugal may have led to the belief that the stigmata of this reputed saint were in some sense an omen of the victory of those arms."

In such cases, when the omen fails, the reaction is always irrational in its violence. Sor Maria was to be vilified as loudly as she had been praised, when her stigmata had been proved to be artificial "and the whole trick invented to gain credit in the world." It is refreshing to find that both these nuns died in genuine sanctity, after having served sentences of enclosure in convents other than those of their respective orders.

One could continue thus through the centuries, and find in each examples of false stigmatics which serve to warn us of the quicksands of this subject. It is not just a matter of fools rushing in, but of wise and learned men advancing cautiously step by step, with the lantern of their investigation held high, who were yet deceived. Fray Luis, provincial superior of the Dominicans in Portugal and a capable professor of theology, pledged his word for the sincerity of Sor Maria, and died quickly from the shock of her exposure.

But, it may be objected, many examples could be gathered from the centuries to show that genuine spiritual phenomena do exist. This is readily admitted: there is St. Francis, and there are saints from St. Catherine of Siena to St. Gemma Galgani who have been marked, in various ways, with the stigmata. But the matter is not closed by admitting this. Caution is supremely needed at every step and in every case.

Hagiographers, in their eagerness to edify, are sometimes too ready to accept "proofs," and it is very instructive to notice how a splendid scholar like Father Thurston picks his way cautiously, watching every word and the undertones and suggestibility of every word. "Stigmatization," he writes (*op. cit.,* p. 70) "is a very wonderful thing, and it is generally found associated with holiness of an exalted kind, but it does not seem in itself to constitute a guarantee of sanctity."

Three things emerge from this: (1) that stigmatization can be genuine; (2) that it is *generally* associated with *exalted* holiness — a double qualification, as our italics show; (3) that stigmatization is not a guarantee of sanctity. A little reflection on this sentence of Thurston's shows that the writer does not intend to belittle stigmatization, but simply to suggest that such *charismata,* such *gratiae gratis datae* may accompany great sanctity, that great sanctity exists without them (our Lady being the supreme example), and anyhow that such things as stigmatization, levitation, penetration of secret thoughts etc. are no final courts of appeal for eminent holiness. Contemporary research into such matters as extrasensory perception and "meta-physical" phenomena strengthens the case for caution.

The Church is supremely cautious when dealing with all such phenomena. Pope Benedict XIV has written the classic work on the canonization of saints, and in it he devotes only a few sentences to stigmatization. He admits, however, that in some rare cases, such as that of St. Francis, stigmatization has a supernatural character.

Man is a strange and wonderful mixture of the angel and the animal, of the spirit and the body. The relations between soul and body, by which the soul acts through the body, create a shadowed region about which we can guess and guess and sometimes be happy in our guesses.

In this region, the laws of nature are sometimes suspended temporarily: wounds appear in hands and feet and side, and the blood continues to defy the laws of nature by flowing upward; levitation occurs, setting Newton and his apple at naught; there is a strange hyperaesthesia of the senses, as when Domenica Lazzari, the Tyrolese "Addolorata" of the last century, heard "what the parish priest said in his sermons delivered in the church 500 or 600 yards away" (Thurston, *op. cit.*, p. 74). In short, it is a region peopled with wonders, and over each wonder the Church has placed a decided question-mark as to its value as an indication for sanctity.

Msgr. Barbier recorded in 1877, that Pope Pius IX said to him: "You write for the press. Say loudly, therefore, and say it often, that the Pope condemns all these visionaries with revelations — Palma, Cantiamille, and the others who deceive the faithful and lead them astray. It is all the work of the devil. I have documents to prove it."

In this region of shadow, the strange shapes that loom up may be the wraiths of pithiatism, i.e. of abnormal suggestibility; or they may be, as Pius IX pointed out so emphatically, the work of the devil who knows how to lead men towards damnation by a spurious show of externals. Or again, from this region of the relation of soul with body, may come genuine physical phenomena which are the outward signs of intense, living union with the crucified Christ.

What, then, is to be said of stigmata in the case of canonized saints? Does canonization declare automatically that all the physical phenomena in the life of the person canonized, were of supernatural origin? Let Father Martindale, S.J. (*The Month,* June, 1952) answer the question for us: "First, canonization does not mean that the Church decides that all the abnormal experiences of a saint were supernatural in origin; in fact, not seldom the Holy See when canonizing a saint has said that it abstains from qualifying such experiences. And secondly, it is not impossible that a saint should suffer from neuroses: indeed, it may be precisely by coping with some such disability that the sufferer wins through to sanctity."

We read in the life of Blessed Gemma Galgani that she warned her confessor, Msgr. Volpi, that a doctor would see nothing if he came to examine her. The confessor insisted on taking a doctor to see her, and the narrative continues: "The doctor took a towel, dipped it in water, and wiped Gemma's hands and forehead. The blood immediately disappeared and the skin showed no signs of cicatrix, scratch, or puncture, as if there had never been any laceration."

Was Gemma a fraud? And has the Church canonized a fraud? It is certainly true that this doctor wiped away the blood and found the skin whole and normal; but it is also true that the reality of her wounds was established beyond dispute on many other occasions. Is it possible, therefore, that Gemma's wounds were sometimes of supernatural origin, sometimes the result of a pathological condition, or indeed a combination of both? Whatever we may think, we can have nothing but admiration for the centuries-wise prudence of the Church, when, in beatifying Gemma Galgani, it explicitly refused to qualify in any way her physical phenomena.

When hysteria can be excluded, and the general tenor of the stigmatic's life gives evidence of high sanctity, the Church admits that a supernatural origin is possible. Beyond that, it will not go.

"With Christ, I am nailed to the Cross," said St. Paul, and there is not the least evidence in patristic writing to show that he meant this to be taken literally. St. Paul uses the words as they might be used by all saints and indeed by all Christians, who are bound to crucify the flesh "with its vices and its concupiscences" on the Golgotha of their own hearts.

For the world in general, the importance of visible stigmata of supernatural origin, given to certain chosen souls among the holy ones of the earth, is that it emphasizes the fact that we were all born to be crucified in the invisible depths of our souls. Our cross will be the weakness of our fallen nature, and the blows of the hammer on the nails will be our incessant efforts to check our evil tendencies, to crucify "the old man" within us that the "new man" may stand up erect in our lives.

The greatest wonder in the life of a genuine stigmatic is not the visible phenomena, but the splendid self-conquest, the interior "stigmata" of the soul, of which the external are the breath-taking evidence. As Michael Hollings put it very well: "The open wounds are not necessary for this nailing; they are only there displayed, as it were, after the nailing of complete surrender has taken place."

"The nailing of complete surrender . . ." that is the acid test. The stigmatic whose wounds have supernatural significance is the person who is already Christ-like through heroically carrying his cross against the slope of his own nature.

The cross of Christ is thrown like a shadow and a challenge on the souls and on the lives of men. With it comes the call: "Take up your cross and follow me." The answer to that call means struggle and blood — and joy of soul; refusal to answer it means the easy way of the downward slope, emptiness and gloom.

Sometimes that shadow comes burningly on certain chosen souls; they are laid prostrate on the ground, as Padre Pio was in the choir of his friary at St. Giovanni Rotondo, and when they rise, they are marked with the wounds of Christ.

It will be clear from the following account of Padre Pio that, while we wonder and are awe-struck at the marvel of the stigmata and the other external phenomena bestowed on him, the greatest wonder of all was the holiness of his life. There can be no possible doubt that, in his case, the stigmata were accompanied by "the nailing of complete surrender."

2. EARLY LIFE AND STIGMATIZATION

The subject of this brief study, Padre Pio da Pietrelcina, was born on May 25, 1887. Pietrelcina is a very small district in the province of Benevento. His parents were Orazio Forgione and Maria Guiseppa, and by modern standards they are generally referred to as having been "ignorant" — because modern standards overlook the deep, natural wisdom that is gained by living close to the soil and to the crops.

They lived in what one American writer has very curiously called "a very rustic country dwelling" — in fact, a cottage — and they eked out an existence on a small holding. As his family increased, Orazio was forced to emigrate for a while, on two occasions, to America, when the holding failed to meet the family's modest needs.

Thus, "along the cool, sequestered vale" of quiet they might have kept "the noiseless tenor of their way," were it not that one of their sons was named Francesco, and that the design of Alverna was traced in advance on his years.

His Italian biographer, Guiseppe de Rossi, wise with the knowledge of what those years did bring, finds the number 5 — the number of the Sacred Wounds of Christ — clamoring their prophecy about Francesco Forgione's cradle. He was born, the author points out, "in the fifth year of the centenary of the birth of Saint Francis, after whom he was named, in the fifth month of the year, the 25th day (5x5), at 5 p.m., in Pietrelcina, a town of five thousand inhabitants. He lived with five Capuchins . . . took the name of Pius V, whose feast occurs on the fifth day in the fifth month of the year. Today, Padre Pio lives with five priests. . . . His cell number is Number 5."

We are used to wonders about the cradles of great men, but this is certainly a bold bid to make a symbolic number dance a prophetic dance. One finds it rather a pity that the writer failed to notice that there are five syllables in Pietrelcina. All this has really as much significance as the fact that Francesco Forgione had five fingers on each hand and the same number of digits on each foot.

But I have seen and heard this, and similar mesmeric passages, quoted as though it in some fashion settled the whole matter in advance. It all savors too much of the horoscope and its wonders; and if cool sanity is to be preserved in our approach, it is vitally necessary to exclude any seeking for portents. They are plentiful enough in the facts of Padre Pio's life.

Father Martindale had pointed out that there is a striking resemblance between the parents of Padre Pio and the parents of Jacinta and Francisco Marto, of Fatima, "even in feature." This is especially so in their simplicity and their pleasant gaiety, their hospitality, deep human and spiritual worth, and that poise between the things of time and the things of eternity which makes vaunted urban elegance appear as the tinsel it is.

There is a tremendous loam of greatness in "the true dignity of the peasant": Vincent de Paul grew from this loam, Julie Billiart grew from it to found the magnificent Congregation of the Sisters of Notre Dame, and it nourished a Joan of Arc and a Genevieve.

It was from this rich soil of human worth that Padre Pio got those qualities which, heightened by the grace of God, were his in their fullness: humility and self-effacement — for the true peasant does not walk this world as though its sides were mirrors reflecting his every movement; tremendous stamina; forthright intolerance of insincerity; and above all, that gaiety which rippled quietly in every feature of his face.

Both his father and his mother died with the hand of their son raised in absolution over them; they have gone, we feel, to contemplate in Beatitude the eternal glory of those Wounds, whose image was traced in the body of their son. That son owed much that was greatest and best in him to the best and greatest in his parents.

We know little of the childhood of Padre Pio. He seems to have been of a quiet and retiring nature, sensitive in a high degree to anything savoring of blasphemy and irreligious thoughtlessness. Some of his biographers serve us up the usual pious stand-by, that he watched the games of his companions rather than joined in them, "thus avoiding arguments and bickerings."

His own description of his childhood as *un macherone senza sale* (an unsalted macaroni) would seem to bear this out. We presume he meant that the "salt" — the rough and tumble — was missing. But it must not be supposed that he was a spineless type of child, for the spineless do not grow into men like Padre Pio. At five, we are told, he dedicated himself to St. Francis. At the age of nine, his mother reported, she found him sleeping on the floor with a stone for a pillow.

For some reason or other, he began by giving the impression of being mentally slow, but this was not the case as he showed later on. As time went on, his education added to the perennial difficulty of making ends meet. A Latin grammar had to be bought, and it cost fourteen *lire*; his education cost five *lire* a month, "the price of half a load of wheat" — "but the boy ate another half-load too."

What all this meant for him was hard and serious work, and for his parents the constant scraping and gathering together of the means to live. His good father used to encourage him by holding before him the hope of the priesthood: "If you learn, I will make you a monk! A Mass-Monk, not a begging-Monk." In 1902, Francesco entered on the way that was to lead to the fulfillment of this promise.

He entered the novitiate of the Capuchin friary at Morcone in the province of Benevento. Here he began those fasts and penances which wore down his body to such an extent that his parents were shocked when they saw him at the end of the year. They asked the *Padre Guardiano* why he was in such a run-down condition, and they were anxious to bring him home; but the padre assured them that what Francesco was eating was little indeed, but quite sufficient for him.

The good parents had great confidence in the Father Guardian, but one feels that they went away far from reassured. Now as Fra Pio, he was transferred to S. Elia a Pianisi, and between each transfer from house to house in the course of his studies, his superiors sent him home to Pietrelcina to recuperate.

It would be wrong to suppose that Fra Pio's superiors were in any way negligent of his health; on the contrary, they took great precautions. At various times he ran high temperatures of up to 106 degrees, but the fever, on the other hand, would leave him with quite startling suddenness.

We are told that, on one occasion, he could not eat for a whole fortnight. His father came, and was sadly bringing him home to die; but he kept feeling better, and ended by having three helpings of turnip when he arrived home.

At Venafro, he lived without food for 21 days, except Holy Communion. During that time, he followed all the exercises of the community. He was persuaded to eat several times, but each time he vomited, "and there returned to his mouth the Host, all intact, which he had received that same morning" (Carty).

It is easy to see how the least wind of this would start the rumor of "a saint," and this is exactly what happened. Because of it, he was again transferred, and Fra Pio had his first experience of how a reputation for sanctity can be in itself a cross.

Fra Pio's student years were marked with prayer, penance, and an attitude of intense reverence towards his studies. He is reported to have been seen many times studying theology on his knees. In those years, moreover, he crossed swords many times with the devil. The most extraordinary case of this known to us from those years of his life, took place in the deep silence of the night.

In a Capuchin friary, the silence of the night is deepened further by the rule of "the great silence" which enjoins that every member shall recollect himself in the deep calm of prayer. He thus creates about him an atmosphere of recollection which is his immediate preparation for morning meditation, as also his guard against the "the evil that prowls in darkness."

One hot summer's night, Fra Pio lay sleepless in his dark cell. Obviously Fra Anastasio in the next cell was also unable to sleep, for Fra Pio could hear him pacing up and down. Fra Pio wished to speak to him, and for this purpose he went to his own open window. He tried to speak, but his throat felt suddenly dry and gritty so that he was unable to make a sound. Then he saw a huge black dog, its fierce eyes staring at him from an enormous head. A second later, it bounded off in a tremendous leap to the roof. Fra Pio lay through that night in great terror, and learned with amazement that Fra Anastasio had not slept there and that the cell had been empty!

On the 10th of May, 1910, Fra Pio became Padre Pio, by being ordained to the priesthood. Ordination is the great central pivotal point in the life of every priest, but it was especially so for Padre Pio. The great centres radiating warmth and meaning through the life of Padre Pio were the Mass and the sacrament of penance. The wonder of his celebration of Mass and the secret heroism of his endless hours in the confessional, overshadow the wonder of his mystical phenomena.

The burning shadow of the Five Wounds was soon to mark him with the stigmata; but the deep meaning of that stigmata was that Padre Pio already bore those wounds lovingly in his heart. The wounds in the body were to mirror the wounds of love in his heart, stamped there by deep recollection in the heart of the Mass.

Padre Pio celebrated his first Mass at Benevento, but very

shortly afterwards he was sent to Pietrelcina, where he remained for some years to help the arch-priest Don Salvatore Pannullo, who was advanced in years. This priest wished to keep him at Pietrelcina, and Padre Pio wrote to Rome asking to be secularized. This request was granted, but Padre Pio remembered that he had dedicated himself to St. Francis in his childhood, and he decided not to make use of the permission.

It is at this stage of his life that we first meet with one of the now well-known facets of the Pio "legend" — the unusual length of his Mass. Typically enough, we first hear of it through a complaint made by the congregation to Don Salvatore. Indeed, it is recorded that the sacristan found him immovable behind the altar, one day, and thought he was dead.

Padre Pio continued to serve the people in Pietrelcina, edifying them by his virtues and irritating some of them by the length of his Mass, till 1915, when an event took place which was to be the beginning of his widespread fame.

Significantly enough, it was the 20th of September, the feast of the Stigmata of St. Francis. Padre Pio had built for himself a little straw hut — after the manner of the Carmelite hermitages — about a hundred yards behind his parent's house. On the day in question, his mother had come to call him for dinner. He emerged from the hut waving his hands like a person who has just been burnt.

"Are you playing an imaginary guitar?" asked his mother with a laugh. He gave her "a curt answer" — the curtness due, perhaps, to the fact that he had experienced something he did not himself quite understand and which, therefore, he was not willing to discuss. We are told that he ate quite a good meal that day. From that time, however, he suffered very severe pains, and Don Salvatore suggested that he should omit the celebration of Mass, "anyhow on Fridays." Padre Pio would not have this.

It is not certain whether Don Salvatore wrote an account of his seven years of deep intimacy with Padre Pio — or, at any rate, such an account, if written, has not been made available. It is certain, however, that he said that Padre Pio told him, on the evening of the feast of St. Francis' Stigmata 1915, that he had received "invisible stigmata," similar to those of St. Catherine of Siena.

For a time, what Goethe called "the commonplace that lays its bond upon us all" hid this moment of breathless wonder. Italy became involved in World War One, and Padre Pio was called up for military service.

This episode in his life comes like one of those moments of comic relief — if the phrase is not irreverent (Padre Pio himself certainly would not have considered it so) — which Shakespeare constantly introduces after a terse scene.

Padre Pio was a splendid, a magnificent soldier of Christ, but he was certainly never cut out for a soldier of any other kind. As though to point up this fact, he was issued a uniform several sizes too big for him, and he lived this short period of his life with all the discomfort of being a misfit.

The uniform was cut too large for him, but there is a sense in which he himself was made on too big a pattern for that uniform. The life which that unifrom signifies is one which has indeed its moments of high heroism; but its ordinary rhythm is low-pulsed, and its language a tissue of irreverence and blasphemy and smut. This must have been a sore trial for a man as sensitive as Padre Pio.

It was established that he was suffering from tuberculosis, and he was sent home from the military hospital at Naples to recuperate for six months. He was then "to await instructions." We cannot blame Padre Pio if he took that order very literally indeed.

When the six months were up, there was a hue and cry out for him as a deserter. Nobody knew where Francesco Forgione was, though a good many people knew that *Padre Pio* was at San Giovanni Rotondo, half-way up the Gargano mountain. The Marshal of Pietrelcina was driven to his wits' end trying to find him, and at last learned from his sister that the elusive Francesco was Padre Pio in San Giovanni.

A house-to-house search caught up at last with Francesco — a smiling Padre Pio who informed his pursuers that now the instructions which he had been told "to await," had at last reached him! A month later, he was discharged with a pension, X-rays having shown that he was suffering from pulmonary tuber-culosis.

We have mentioned San Giovanni Rotondo in passing, and we must now return to concentrate for a moment on this spot which has since become a place of pilgrimage. The climb by road to San Giovanni gives a magnificent view of the Adriatic, and there is a wealth of luxuriant vegetation — olive trees, holm oak, chestnut, and everywhere the vine, bent down with its load of grapes, promising an abundance of wine.

Some distance from the town stands the Capuchin friary, once famous as the place where St. Camillus de Lellis made his noviti-ate, and now famous as the home of Padre Pio. He came there in 1916, and two years later the marvel occurred of his complete visible stigmata of which his earlier experience in his little straw hut had been but the beginning.

Again it was the feast of the Stigmata of St. Francis. On the Friday within the octave — the 20th of September, 1918 — shortly before noon, a sharp cry of pain was heard from the choir in the chapel, where Padre Pio was kneeling in prayer. His fellow-priests hurried to the choir, and found him prostrate on the ground as though he had been mysteriously struck down.

Strange wounds were found in his hands, feet and side, and blood was pouring from them. The great crucifix above him, from which, we are told, the piercing darts of elective love had come, looked down on the scene. And the eyes of Padre Pio were raised to his brethren, filled with a plea for their silence.

His brethren lifted him and carried him to his cell.

3. HIS FAME GOES ABROAD

Years before he received the visible stigmata, Padre Pio was drawing crowds to him; it was this very fact, as well as consideration for his health, which led his superiors to choose for him the tiny, secluded friary of San Giovanni Rotondo.

From the very first, he seems to have had a thirst for ministering to souls through the sacrament of penance, and his spiritual genius in knowing how to comfort his penitents and send them away happy in the peace of grace, was as a magnet drawing souls to him. Superiors of religious bodies are very prudent men, and they are wisely concerned to avoid, if at all possible, limelight and the buzz of excited voices.

Wherever Padre Pio went, the same great thirst for souls was felt in him, and souls flocked to his confessional to satisfy that thirst and to feel the peace he could bring them. Padre Pio, as Piera Sessa remarks, wished to be considered not as a wonder, not as a stigmatic, but as a confessor. This was true of his years of priesthood before his stigmatization, and it remained so afterwards.

When we think of the mystical gift of stigmatization given to a holy man, we imagine it as something which surrounds him with the hush of reverence and which brings the faithful of every nation to sit at his feet in awe. This, of course, is true; and, as we shall

19

see, was very true indeed of Padre Pio. But it is only part of the picture.

We are inclined to forget that the gift is the splendid, visible image of Christ's wounds, and that those wounds are in the pattern of the Cross. The essence of the gift, therefore, is that it comes as the blessing of a cross to the chosen one.

Padre Pio's most ardent wish — always deferring, of course, to God's wishes for him — was that he should be allowed to continue his great privilege of lifting the Hand of Christ over penitents, in the darkness and obscurity of his confessional. But it pleased God that the veil of his hiding-place should be rent, and that the lime-light of pious enthusiasm should come on him.

It is the hall-mark of the genuine quality of his holiness that he accepted all this in simplicity; and, since humility is the touch-stone in all these matters, the readiness with which he submitted to vexatious medical examinations, and to the Roman decision which had the effect of barring him temporarily from his beloved confessional, is a greater glory than his stigmata. Indeed, the latter would have no significance without it.

The smiling face of Padre Pio was the face of Franciscan sim-plicity. It was with this simplicity that Padre Pio received the gift of the cross, and effaced himself all the more because of the gift. In this, as in everything else, he was at one with the heart of his master St. Francis, who ended his wonderful *Laudes Creaturarum* with the lines:

> "Laudate e benedicite lu mi signore et rengratiate
> Et serviateli cum grande humiliate. Amen."

"Praise and bless my Lord, and give him thanks, and serve him with great humility. Amen." (*St. Francis of Assisi, Writings and Early Biographies,* p. 131.)

But the quiet finality of that *Amen* — the submissively joyful *So be it* of humility — was not for Padre Pio. From being a rela-tively obscure Capuchin friar in one of the tiniest friaries of his order, he had become a challenge to medicine and to all its laws, and a light of wonder to the faithful in every part of the world.

Moreover, he was now a "problem child," so to speak, of Mother Church — for he was presenting the phenomena of complete male stigmatization which had not occurred since St. Francis of Assisi. (See Thurston, *op. cit.*, p. 109). All of these gave their own answers to "the case of Padre Pio."

Medicine came forward first in the person of Doctor Luigi Romanelli di Barletta, who had been invited by the Father Provincial to make an examination. The important items of his conclusions were: "that the wounds are not superficial"; "the blood is arterial in character"; "the lesions on the hands are covered with a thin membrane, reddish brown in color, with no bleeding points, no swelling, no inflammation of the tissue"; "the tissues around the lesions . . . are painful even to a light touch."

Romanelli sums up: "I saw Padre Pio five times in the course of fifteen months. I found some modifications, but I have nothing which enables me to make an authoritative classification of these wounds." He describes his experiment on the stigmatic as "seeming barbarous" — "I repeated this seeming barbarous experiment several times in the evening . . . and in the morning."

When we realize that it consisted of pressing his fingers to the front and back of the wound, and exploring for a gap such as would suggest complete transfixion; and when we remember that we have the doctor's own word for the hyper-sensitivity of these regions, we begin to have some idea of just what this gift of stigmatization meant to Padre Pio. He must have suffered intensely from this examination; and we must emphasize that he submitted to it all cheerfully and without the least complaint.

Romanelli was followed in July, 1919, by Professor A. Bignami, an agnostic of the Roman University. He reversed the decision by stating that the wounds *were* superficial.

Padre Pio had been advised to use iodine "to cauterize, if possible, the wounds, and to protect them against infection." Bignami based an objection on this, but later dropped it when Padre Pio began to use a coarse soap and ordinary water. The iodine had been absolutely ineffectual.

Bignami seems to have come to Padre Pio with the same attitude which Zola brought to Lourdes — and his conclusions ruled out the supernatural in advance. There could be no denying the wounds, but he minimized their significance to the utmost by pronouncing them "superficial," a matter on which Romanelli was later to take him up.

He concluded that the lesions were due "to a necrosis of the epidermis of neurotic origin," and their cruciform arrangement "probably attributable to unconscious suggestion." There was nothing there, in his opinion, that could not be attributed to natural causes.

The next to examine him was Doctor G. Festa of Rome, in October, 1919. The agnostic Bignami had come down heavily on the side of a natural explanation, but he admitted fully that apart from the hyperaesthesia of the parts surrounding the lesions, his meticulous examination had discovered no trace of the neurotic, in any shape or form, in Padre Pio.

There were, however, what Festa called "many inaccuracies" in his report, and this made Festa decide to return accompanied by Dr. Romanelli. They established fully that "the scabs or pellicules on the lesions are crusts of dried blood, which when removed show the actual wounds, continually bleeding."

This time, one is relieved for the good Padre's sake, to read that no attempt was made to determine the depth of the wound, "owing to the hyper-sensitivity of the surrounding tissue."

They concluded that the wounds were a "true and proper lesion of the *continuum,* deep as if made by a pointed instrument." This conclusion may be said to have been established.

Suggestions were not wanting to explain away the supernatural by explaining the phenomenon as a natural one. Hemophilia was at hand to explain all, of course — until, as we shall see, it was established that other wounds in his body went through a perfectly normal process of healing.

Hysteria was suggested, but the conclusive answer seems to have been that Padre Pio was a perfectly normal man — "genial, humorous and apparently most *un*-impressionable," is Father Martindale's summary of the impression he makes on all — and therefore not unduly subject to neuroses. The matter need not be pressed any further.

Certainly those writers on Padre Pio do their cause no good, who stress the absence of symptoms of hysteria as conclusive of anything. The conquering of neuroses may be the means through which a soul attains to sanctity and the presence of such neuroses does *not,* per se, exclude the possibility of genuinely spiritual physical phenomena.

Though the eminent neuropathologist, Babinski asserts that hysteria has *never* produced lesions of the skin, it is highly dangerous to make a definitive statement where one is dealing with that mysterious region of the soul's action on the body.

Most of the doctors and psychiatrists whom Father Martindale questioned in his researches, "now say that 'hysteria' *can* produce organic lesions, but none, so far, has offered an example of this happening" (*vide* his absorbing article in *The Clergy Review,* November, 1952).

That no example has been given proves nothing, and certainly does not warrant any sweeping statement. "I could not feel surprised," says Father Martindale, "if we were shown that we are still very far from knowing to what extent the mind can modify matter."

One sentence from his article is worth isolating as a sane summary of the whote matter: "Stigmata *may* be both supernatural (in their ultimate cause) and natural as effects (in a holy person, foreseen and permitted by God.) "

Perhaps if Padre Pio could have assembled all the disputants together, he might quite conceivably have shouted for silence, and then have read over them that chapter from the *Imitation*: "On Searching into High Matters."

It would have been a typically humorous touch from the man who, when he might have been expected to utter profundities about the origin of his religious vocation, said simply: "I always liked bearded religious, and so became a Capuchin."

Year followed year, and Padre Pio lived peacefully in his friary, giving himself to the ministry of the confessional, and leaving the controversies about him to others. He was adept at doing this, as he showed in his calm answer to the somewhat acid question of Doctor Bignami.

Feeling somewhat balked at the end of his examination, and as an unbeliever finding it hard to stomach the whole affair; knowing too, that the importance he had attached to the Padre's use of iodine could carry no weight, he asked:

"Tell me, Father, why did your wounds appear in these places and not in other parts of your body?"

"You are the man of science, Doctor," came the quiet reply, "perhaps *you* can tell me why they should have appeared in other parts of my body and not in these parts?"

Pope Benedict XV was very well disposed towards Padre Pio. He is recorded to have said: "Padre Pio is indeed an extraordinary man. He is one of those whom God sends from time to time to earth to convert mankind." This was in 1921, and it fixed the ecclesiastical attitude to Padre Pio as a benevolent one.

In October, 1924, however, came a special issue of the periodical: *Vita e Pensiero,* in honor of the seventh centenary of St. Francis' stigmata. It carried an article by the famous Father Gemelli O.F.M., then at the height of his theological fame, where, dealing with the case of Padre Pio, he said that as the lesions "which are described in him reveal a damaged condition in the tissues in which they occur" — as distinguished from what he called the "flesh nails" of St. Francis of Assisi — "it is possible to regard them as derived from a morbid state, from a psychopathic condition, or else as the effect of actual stimulation."

These were hard words, and Doctor Festa came forward quickly with a scientific reply. The Jesuit *Civilta Catholica* censured Gemelli's article as "inexact and imprudent," but the matter rested at that.

In 1923, the Holy Office (A.A.S., July 5th) had spoken, its *non constare*: the phenomena appertaining to Padre Pio could not be affirmed with certainty to be supernatural. But in 1924, the attitude of Rome became yet more cautious. Then and again in 1931, certain books about him were forbidden, and the faithful were forbidden to go on pilgrimage to him or to write to him. Padre Pio was forbidden to say Mass in public, and he was no longer permitted to hear confessions or to preach.

In 1925, the Holy Office also sent an "extraordinary commissary" to San Giovanni, and caused him to be elected superior of all the Capuchin friaries in the province of Foggia. But this priest soon became a defender of Padre Pio's virtues and great prerogatives.

Father Martindale wrote in 1952 that he did "not know whether the veto upon his activities was explicitly revoked: he still may not preach, and his confreres have had even recently to curb the legend that is growing up about his alleged prophecies" (*The Month*).

It is also of interest to note how that vigilance over popular hysteria continued. Six books on Padre Pio were put on the Index in 1952 because they were published without an *Imprimatur*. It was made clear, however, that this involved no reflection either on the integrity of Padre Pio or of the writers.

From the very beginning, Padre Pio had been a pious "sensation," and Rome is always wary of such. He himself did nothing to attract the pious to him: he wanted sinners, and he wanted them in the confessional where he could exercise in Christ's name the power of forgiving sin, of lifting up the weary and the broken.

Still the pilgrims behaved sometimes in an exited and far from edifying way. "As soon as Padre Pio reached the vesting table, people began to press forward to touch him. They almost prevented him from vesting for Mass, and when they began to get out of hand he became very stern and told them to leave him alone. . . ." "Now and then there were slightly heated arguments outside the 'box' as to whose turn it was next. . . ." (*The Universe*, Dec. 12, 1952).

Padre Pio stood up in our modern world as a living image of the Crucified. We have much to learn from his humility and his holiness. What a pity his name had to be surrounded by such pious emotional hysteria, however much that hysteria was counter-balanced by the sanity and the reverence of those who went to San Giovanni in a spirit of quiet devotion. But, like the poor, I suppose the intoxicated pious will be always with us.

4. "THE ODOR OF SANCTITY"

"We are the good odor of Christ unto God," wrote St. Paul in his second letter to the Corinthians (2, 15). The old hagiographers established the fact that when a man's holiness causes him to become a veritable vessel of that "good odor," he may give off an aroma which is very inspiring but usually has no recognized affinity with any known pleasant odor of spices or perfumes or flowers. This, when the phrase is taken literally, is what is meant by "the odor of sanctity."

Modern hagiographers fight shy of it, because it has become a cliché in the hands of those pious writers who have changed it into a metaphorical phrase so that all their subjects may die in "the odor of sanctity."

On the other hand, the chronicler describing the removal of the hairshirt from the dead body of Saint Thomas à Becket, says that the vermin "boiled over like water in a simmering cauldron" (see MacArthur, *Old Time Typhus in Britain*). Saint Thomas — "the hooly blisful martir," as Chaucer called him — was a great saint, for hygiene and odors have nothing essentially to do with sanctity. There are unwashed scoundrels and perfumed saints; there are unwashed saints and perfumed scoundrels.

It is absolutely non-essential that sanctity should have an odor of any kind. There is historical evidence, however, that it some-

27

times does give off a strange aroma. This was more often than not, associated with the dead body of the saint, as, for example, when St. Anthony climbed to the platform of the column on which St. Simeon Stylites lived, and found the saint's dead body "exhaling the perfume as it were of many spices." Here the perfume is compared to a rather vague odor of "many spices" which does not help to identify it.

Testimony concerning this same odor emanating from a *living* person is much more rare. There is, for example, the famous scent "as of violets," according to one nun, but absolutely unidentifiable, according to others, which emanated from the person of St. Catherine de Ricci at certain times in her life. There is no valid reason why the testimony in her case, and in some others, may not be believed.

We can take it that the fact of this perceptible, mysterious odor, is established as one of the physical phenomena of holiness while in no way essential to holiness — unless of course we are indeed as Chesterton's dog Quoodle so gloriously described us: "Even the smell of roses is not what they supposes, They do not trust their noses. . . ."

But while we accept the possibility and historical occurrence of the phenomenon, great care must be taken not to accept the testimony of every nose. Color, according to one school of philosophy, is in the eye of the beholder; in much of the testimony to the odor of sanctity, we may well suggest that the perfume was in the nose of the inhaler! With this *caveat,* we turn to the phenomenon as reported of Padre Pio.

If we accept the probably supernatural character of Padre Pio's stigmata — and there seems as much compelling reason for doing so as we can look for, remembering that warning of Aristotle that we must expect "only that certainty which the nature of the subject permits" — it seems a small matter indeed to believe that the lesions gave off a pleasing and strange odor.

I cannot speak from experience — I did not experience that odor, nor have many of the pilgrims with whom I have discussed

it. On the weight of published evidence, however, I am prepared
to accept the fact that there was such an odor — though I wish
the matter could be left at that, and I were not asked to believe,
as one American writer asked us, that it was "especially the odor
of violets, lilies, roses, incense, or even fresh tobacco."

Perhaps, perhaps — but please do not let me get "the odor of
sanctity" confused with that Virginian aroma which greets me at
my tobacconist. It is well that we have the direct testimony of
a man like Doctor Festa to rely on. His testimony is as follows:

"I testify that on my first visit, I took from his side a small,
bloodstained cloth which I brought back to Rome for microscopic
examination. As I am myself entirely deprived of the sense of
smell, I did not get any special odor from it.

"But a distinguished official and other persons who were with
me on my return to Rome from San Giovanni, and who knew
nothing of that piece of cloth in my case, experienced a very
strong perfume in spite of the rush of air, and they assured me
that it was exactly like the perfume they had caught from the
person of Padre Pio.

"At Rome, in the following days and for a long time to come,
my study was filled with a perfume emanating from that piece of
cloth in my cabinet, so much so that many of my patients asked
what was the strange odor."

This odor was so pronounced, we are told, that a lady who
hesitated between two Doctor Festa's in the telephone directory,
walked to one of them and knew she had chosen the right one
because the odor of Padre Pio greeted her through the open door.

We may add to this the evidence of an unbeliever confrère of
Doctor Festa who wondered, when he left him, why a man of
such reputed holiness should trifle with perfumes.

One more testimony is that of the author, Alberto Dei Fante,
biographer of Padre Pio. One night in February, 1931, he decided,
as writers do when they find that the ink of inspiration is flowing
freely, to sit up very late over his work. He had just begun to get
"dug in," with the silence of the sleeping house about him, when

he noticed a strange perfume filling his room. He recognized it as that of Padre Pio — and he immediately remembered that, contrary to his promise to the padre, he had not begun his work with the Sign of the Cross.

Parente (*op. cit.*, p. 55) has called this odor "the voice of the blood" — the means by which Padre Pio communicates with those whom he wishes to guide or who in any way are intimately linked with him through the mysterious channels of prayer. But once again, let us reach for the good garment of caution. We shall record some of the evidence that has been brought forward, and it will be admitted that some of it is naive in the extreme.

On the strength of Doctor Festa's words, I am prepared to accept the reality of the strange perfume from the lesions of Padre Pio. *Per se,* there is no reason why that odor should not make itself felt if God so wills that it should do so. Yet in these matters the human imagination can play strange pranks, and however solidly we may think our feet are placed on the ground, we are liable to illusions in all good faith.

Let us instance a few parallels. An eminent English critic — I think it was Drinkwater — once wrote that if, when shaving, a particularly powerful line of poetry came to his mind, his blood raced, his eyes dimmed, his skin became hypersensitive, and he invariably cut himself. I know another, a musician, who stoutly maintains that a note at a certain pitch puts a fog of green before his eyes, another note a haze of vivid orange, another a light filagree of red, and so forth.

And when we leave the *savants* and enter the world of the common man, what a wealth of stories we find, what a phantasmagoria of goblins and ghosts and fairies and "good people" in a mist of Celtic or Welsh or Breton or any other twilight you please!

From there, pass on to the strange antics of men under the stress of religious enthusiasm — the world of Msgr. Knox's book: *Enthusiasm,* and one becomes very wary indeed of that "voice of the blood" inhaled in Genoa, Milan, Venice, and — perhaps — even in Broadway.

As an example of the evidence brought forward, take this sentence from Father Carty's book: *Padre Pio, the Stigmatist* (p. 60) : "Very often the phenomenon is manifested among groups of persons intent on speaking about the great Capuchin." Once again, there is no *per se* reason why that should not have been so; but that *intent on speaking* conjures up the picture of an earnest, somewhat excited group who might imagine anything. Perhaps, on the contrary, they were a group of calm, sage people; but anyhow, it all happened "very often."

Turning to Father Parente's book for some better evidence, we meet with the same vague generalities. "It has been attested by *many witnesses worthy of belief* that this characteristic perfume has *often* been perceived hundreds of miles from San Giovanni Rotondo, where Padre Pio now spends all his time."

The italics are ours, and they certainly call for comment. In the first place, the whole sentence is vague, for it leaves us wondering who made up this multitude of witnesses. Surely the phenomenon was not of such common occurrence that it warranted both a *many* and an accelerating *often* in the same sentence?

To adopt a metaphor from that immensely sane founder of the Assumption Family, Emmanuel d'Alzon, writers of such sentences are like postillions who whip up their horses to such a convincing gallop that they risk the horses' necks. It is not good to be too eager in making one's point. Again, why is *distance* brought in to strengthen the case? After all, here, as in every other wonder, *c'est le premier pas qui coûte.*

Turning now to the specific evidence, what intrinsic conviction does it carry? We are told of a group of women "on the fifth floor of an apartment in the heart of Genoa" — such precise location, one must presume, strengthens the testimony — who were discussing Padre Pio, when suddenly there came "a wave of the characteristic fragrance of violets."

The writer goes on to say that others present, "even though

they possessed a perfect sense of smell," did not notice the perfume. This last point is apparently brought forward as conclusive evidence of the spiritual reality of the perfume. It might be equally conclusive of the opposite.

There have been saints who saw visions, as St. Bernadette did at Lourdes, while thousands present saw nothing. We believe the visions of St. Bernadette because there is a whole world of scientific evidence to warrant our believing.

But there are also the Hamlets who point with frantic conviction at nothing; and — to descend to a "phenomenon" we all know only too well — there is the old, or not so old woman who sees the headless man at the crossroads, and there are the *many* who see it after their imaginations have been sufficiently kindled, and their nerves sufficiently set on edge, by the recital.

I have before me a wealth of testimony to the experience of this odor, the mysterious promptings of this "voice of the blood." It is not convincing.

"How can it be an illusion if it reaches great and unexpected distances?" asks Father Carty (*op. cit.*, p. 59). Surely this is to beg the whole question. The very fact of its alleged reaching to such distances, so far from being a proof that it is *not* an illusion, is an added caution that perhaps it may be. In the present state of the evidence, the possibility of illusion cannot be ruled out.

Theresa Neumann, as Friedrich Ritter von Lama tells us, had a sudden vision of St. Mary Magdalen setting off in a sail-less, rudderless boat, and running into a storm.

We have all heard the legend of the voyage of Saints Mary Magdalen, Lazarus, Martha and others across the Mediterranean. Are we to set aside the learned evidence of the *Lexikon für Theologie und Kirche,* edited by Dr. Michael Buchberger, Theresa's own bishop, and quoted by Father Thurston, that the legend is "altogether unhistorical"?

But, on Father Carty's reasoning, Theresa cannot have been suffering from an illusion. For — how could it have been an illusion if it came to her from "such great and unexpected distances" of time and of space!

To sum up: It seems reasonable to accept as an established fact that there was a strange aroma from the lesions of Padre Pio, and that this aroma was sometimes met with in the church of San Giovanni Rotondo and in the vicinity of his person.

After that, I think some form of Occam's razor — that fine edged *non sunt multiplicanda* — must be called upon to remove those excretions which do great credit to the heart but little to the head.

5. THE GIFT OF BILOCATION

Bilocation is the gift of being present in two different places at the same time. It is a physical phenomenon that has been claimed for some of the saints, for example Saint Anthony of Padua and Saint Alphonsus Liguori. This phenomenon has been claimed for Padre Pio, and the weight of acceptable evidence seems to substantiate that claim.

Above all, there is the reported evidence of his own words on the matter, which we do not possess with regard to the distant appearance of "the odor." All his biographers report a conversation which he had with one of his brethren about bilocation.

"When the phenomenon occurs," his companion suggested, "it is possible that the saints are not really aware of it."

"Oh yes, they are," Padre Pio replied with firm conviction. "They may be uncertain whether the body or the soul goes, but they are certainly aware of what is happening and of where they are going."

Padre Pio would have spoken with such conviction only from personal experience. Only when he was certain of what he was saying did he speak with such emphasis. These words, therefore, may be taken as indisputable evidence that he did possess such a gift, for only by personal experience could one speak with certainty on such a matter.

It would have been completely out of character with Padre Pio, were he to have done so in any other circumstances, for he was "a just man" in the full Scriptural meaning of the word. These words of his make us turn with greater confidence to the evidence that has been gathered from many sources concerning this gift of his.

An Italian work: *Padre Pio da Pietrelcina* by Piera Delfina Sessa, devotes a somewhat long chapter to this matter. Padre Pio, it would appear, was seen praying at the tomb of Pope Pius XI, whom he venerated above all the popes because he was so very simple, so very humble, so very Christ-like in his meekness. This is an interesting side-light on the character of Padre Pio himself, for we tend to reveal our own qualities in the qualities we admire in others.

Sessa also tells us that he was seen "by a saintly bishop at the beatification of Thérèse de Lisieux in St. Peter's, Rome.

On both occasions, he was humbly following his daily routine in the friary at San Giovanni.

There was also the strange case in the Magurno di Diamante family, which adds the second element said to be connected with this gift of Padre Pio — his healing power.

Mrs. Ersilia Magurno had been nursing her husband for two months, and it seemed to doctors and attendants that he would certainly die. A specialist declared that his heart would certainly not stand up to the strain and that he had only a few hours to live.

A telegram had been dispatched to Padre Pio urgently calling for his help, and he had sent an answer at once. In spite of that, the good man seemed to be sinking rapidly towards the grave, but his wife did not lose hope. She felt that Padre Pio was wrestling in prayer for her intention, and her faith in him was stronger than her faith in doctors' words.

She intensified her own prayer, and sent another telegram to Padre Pio. Shortly after this, the patient fell asleep after a very troubled day. To her great joy, he was sleeping peacefully, though he had a temperature of 102 degrees that night. Early the following morning, she asked him:

"How are you feeling?"

"I am feeling splendid," he replied. "Padre Pio has just left me."

"Are you serious?" she asked eagerly. "What did you say? Did you see Padre Pio? What did he tell you?"

"He had a Brother with him. First he examined my heart, and said: 'This temperature will pass and tomorrow you will be all right. After four days you will leave your bed.' Then he looked around, examined the medicines, read the charts, and remained in the room for the rest of the night."

Five months later, the account goes on, the couple drove to San Giovanni Rotondo to thank Padre Pio. Magurno recognized at once the man who had cured him. Greeting him in a friendly and paternal manner, Padre Pio said: "What a deal of trouble that heart of yours gave you!"

One aspect of this case is, that the room in which this strange visit of bilocation occurred was said to have had, in the morning, that distinctive odor associated with the lesions of Padre Pio.

The fact does not weaken what we have said earlier concerning this "odor of sanctity." Apparently, when this phenomenon of bilocation occurs, his "spirit presence," if we may risk a term for it, is sufficiently real to cause this odor. This is quite a different matter from that of the disembodied odor of sanctity for which much unconvincing evidence is put forward.

There have been even more spectacular wonders recorded of him. We are told that during and after the war, many soldiers came to San Giovanni to thank Padre Pio for his help.

We select the case of a pilot who — according to the account of Piera Delfino Sessa — had a very strange experience. He saw a Capuchin rush forward to his assistance and prevent him from falling to his death because of a parachute which would not open.

The pilot's mother had great faith in the prayers of Padre Pio, and had recommended her son to him when he joined the forces. When her son returned, she wanted to send him immediately to Padre Pio to thank him as the Capuchin who had saved his life. The pilot did not know Padre Pio, and he naturally hesitated about putting himself into a position that might prove ridiculous.

"Mother, what are you asking me to do?" he protested. "You know I don't really believe such things can happen."

He finally gave in to his mother, and went, somewhat bewildered by it all, to San Giovanni. As soon as Padre Pio saw him entering the sacristy, he asked:

"Where is my lost lamb? — Where is it?" — and the young man rushed forward to kneel at the feet of the Capuchin who had saved him. He was seeing Padre Pio's face for the first time, and he knew it as the face of the man who had come so mysteriously to him in his time of greatest need.

"Do you remember," continued Padre Pio, "that deadly danger you ran into at Trento? And another time also? . . ."

It must have been a moment of tremendous emotion for this young man.

It has been questioned whether these instances are really cases of bilocation at all, since we have no evidence that Padre Pio was in his friary at the time they occurred. Domenico Argentieri, for instance, has ruled out the word bilocation altogether, and has left us to choose the term *flight, translation, ecstatic transport,* or some other term which expresses miraculous presence without the implication of bi-presence.

Once again, let it be stressed that the real case for this phenomenon rests on those words we have quoted from the Father himself; for they have been repeated so often that it would have been his duty to disown them if they were not his. He never did so, and we may therefore accept them as establishing the phenomenon, even while we maintain the utmost caution with regard to the instances brought forward.

Perhaps a safe guide would be to admit for consideration only those cases about which Padre Pio himself, however indirectly, has had something to say, *provided* these cases have been published in an account to which an *Imprimatur* is attached, and which deserves to be considered seriously. The *Imprimatur,* of course, is not a guarantee of the veracity of such accounts.

Let us isolate here a case which seems clearly to fulfill these three conditions we have suggested.

The Countess Virginia Sili of Rome had all in readiness for the consecration of her oratory. Her guests were around her, and among them were no less personages — Father Carty tells us — than Cardinal Gaspari, her cousin, and Cardinal Sili, her brother-in-law. The question arose as to what saint the oratory was to be dedicated. "A novice ended their discussion," writes Father Carty, "when she entered holding in her hands a reliquary containing a relic of the Holy Cross, and told the following story:

" 'Last night there appeared to me in flesh and bones Padre Pio, who consigned to me this relic, bidding me to bring it to the Countess in the morning before the consecration of the chapel' " (Carty, *Padre Pio,* p. 76). It appears that the Countess had confirmation of this a few days later from Padre Pio himself, when she went to see him.

But to return to the term "bilocation." It is certainly true that in such instances as the above, the fact that they occurred at night makes it impossible to say whether they involved bilocation in the strict sense of the word.

It is straining a point, however, to rule out bilocation while admitting ecstatic flight, for surely it would be more in conformity with his rule of life as a Capuchin — and therefore more in conformity with the Wisdom of God in His dealings with Padre Pio — that he should be in his cell at night even while being also elsewhere to answer a prayer or to be the bearer of a grace.

Furthermore, there have been biographers of Padre Pio who maintain that he was sometimes in three different places at one and the same time — a phenomenon for which the term *pluriloca-tion* has been rather unhappily suggested.

There is nothing strange in this, for, as Blessed Martin de Porres so simply put it when asked to explain the wonder in his own case: "Christ multiplied the loaves and fishes, so what's to prevent Him from multiplying Martin de Porres."

A difficulty arises, however, if we regard such "multiplication" of simultaneous presences as phenomena of ecstatic flight. If Padre Pio was seen in places A, B, and C, presumably he was also at D — the place of his ordinary existence; or else the latter *was* A, B, or C, and therefore only two of the appearances were phenomena. They could not all three be such, and the real Padre Pio just cease to exist for the moment.

In the case of apparent bilocation at night, a case can certainly be made for possible ecstatic flight not involving bilocation. As soon as pulrilocation is brought in, however, complications arise which lead back to bilocation in the first instance.

There is nothing complicated about supposing that Padre Pio remained where his rule says he should have been at any given time, even while what we have called his "spirit presence" was seen in one, two, three, or any number of places elsewhere. For the conformity of a religious to his rule is something which takes precedence of all physical phenomena, as St. Anthony demonstrated for all time when he ordered St. Simeon Stylites to descend from his pillar, and then revoked the order when the saint began immediately to come down.

I think we may take it for granted that God, in His dealings with Padre Pio, respected His own Will for Padre Pio as expressed in the Capuchin rule. To the question, therefore: "Where was Padre Pio in any case of his apparent bilocation or plurilocation?" — the answer may be safely given: "He was where his rule says he should be." Otherwise, all the wonders told of him would be of absolutely no spiritual significance.

Many instances of this strange power of his have been put on record: there was the child, who, inspired in some way beforehand of the time of his coming, told her parents, who mistakenly went to meet him at the railway station, and returned to find he had already visited and cured their child.

There was also that other somewhat disingenuous child who, having been cured by him in similar fashion, thought to test him by feigning her malady, and was gently rebuked by him "not to tempt God's mercy."

There was his voice suddenly thundering "Enough!" over the heads of some soldiers who were plundering the house of a young lady teacher wrongfully accused of having been involved in a Fascist crime, and saving her from the firing squad.

There was the young Roman who abstained from his usual habit of lifting his hat when passing a church, because he had some friends with him who might have smiled. He heard Padre Pio's voice incisively in his ear with the accusing word — "Coward."

Instances could go on and on. In all these cases, we have some creditably reported confirmation by Padre Pio. Sometimes this is spiced with quite delicious wit, as when he said to the Roman when they met: "Next time it will be a sound box on the ear"; and to the teacher saved from the firing squad: "Your faith in invoking my help certainly made me run far enough that time!"

Such humor predisposes us to accept Padre Pio for the great and simple man that he was.

6. THE MASS OF PADRE PIO

When the holiness of a stigmatic gives reason for attributing a supernatural origin to the physical phenomena — as was the case with Padre Pio — his wounds link him in a privileged manner with Christ on the hill of Calvary. It is natural, therefore, that in any account of a stigmatic, great attention should be given to him in relation to the Holy Mass.

It is the present writer's intention to do justice to the undoubted wonders that cluster about the name of Padre Pio; but the reader must be patient if the voice of the commonplace, so to speak, keeps interrupting to recall some dusty facts of our drab lives.

It is too easy to rhapsodize about spiritual wonders, when those wonders take visible shape and touch us on the shoulder. But if the wonder of Padre Pio's stigmata, and the glory of his Mass, are to have real spiritual significance, they must recall us to the unseen spiritual glories that do not have visible shape.

To put it very crudely — I have known some who returned from assisting at the Mass of Padre Pio, and the only positive effect it seems to have had was that they considered themselves then in a position to criticize the manner in which their parish priest celebrated his Mass; whereas, in reality, they might well have returned with a deeper insight into the great *Mysterium* and a more vivid realization that they were returning to the same wonder in their own parish church.

What then, was it like to assist at the Mass of Padre Pio? It was to kneel still before the Mystery, which seemed carried to you as it were through the very wounds in the body of the celebrant, and brought home in the warmth of his fervor.

It made you feel how thickly the dust has settled on your ideas of the supernatural: how, above all, the Mass had become blurred, void of dynamic meaning, in the busy hum of life's highway.

The Mass of Padre Pio jolted men to the realization that the world is too much with us; that we must take steps to remove the dust of neglect from those spiritual wonders that are ours to command. There was a calm renewal of one's sense of the wonder at the *Mysterium Fidei,* everywhere and especially in one's own prosaic parish church.

The secret of the power which the Mass of Padre Pio exercised over all present, can be humanly explained — if explained at all — by the fact that the drama inherent in the Mass makes itself more vividly felt through the celebrating priest.

A famous Catholic dramatist once wrote (*Catholic Herald,* March 25, 1949): "It is, I think, significant that Catholicism is in itself theatrical in the very highest sense of the word. The confessional is a stage shrouded in sombre curtains of tragedy, with one divine spotlight; the Stations of the Cross are an episodic drama of overwhelming emotions; the Blessed Eucharist is a sublime and flawless poem; the Holy Mass is the greatest classical drama that ever was written."

The spiritual catharsis that the Mass can effect is more dramatically felt when it comes to us through a great priest. For, as Father Petitot has reminded us (*Introduction to Holiness,* p. 92 — English translation), the priest exercises an art: "A very fervent priest, a saint, by his manner of reciting public prayers, of genuflecting, of prostrating, of chanting, of attending to the least rubrics, practices excellently, though he may not be conscious of it, religious art. . . . When it is appreciated that the prayers of the Mass make, so to speak, a sacred poem of simple and divine sublimity, it is easy to understand that the priest who, without being a Curé d'Ars, celebrates Mass piously, reverently, and religiously, performs a work which is not only of infinite value, but also of incomparable aesthetic worth."

Now, if this is so when the celebrant is our parish priest and the emotional atmosphere is that of the nine o'clock Mass on a wet Sunday morning, we can appreciate how the drama of it all was immensely heightened when the priest was a famous stigmatic, when people had come from far-off lands to assist at the Mass and when spiritual emotions ran high.

The first distinguishing feature of the Mass of Padre Pio was its length, varying between an hour and a quarter and an hour and a half. The audible parts of the Mass, however, were said just as any other priest would have said them; there was no hint of dramatic resonance in his voice or any slow emphasis. The length of his Mass was due to the long pauses of contemplative silence into which he entered at various parts of the Holy Sacrifice.

When he first approached the altar, before reading the Introit, he made a considerable pause before the tabernacle as though in contemplation of the mighty work he was about to perform.

The celebration of Mass seemed to mean pain and suffering for Padre Pio, and sometimes a little trickle of blood was seen to flow from the wounds in his hands. He always put a handkerchief on the altar for such moments. Is it fanciful to see an analogy here between that first moment of Padre Pio's Mass and the moment when Christ first faced His passion? Was there something of the shadow of Gethsemane on the soul of Padre Pio in that silence before the tabernacle?

After the *Orate Fratres* he again stood silently as he savored, perhaps, the deep significance of that *meum ac vestrum sacrificium*.

This was followed by a long pause at the memento of the living, for Padre Pio had many to remember. The sorrows of the world all came to him, and he accepted them as his own. In that deep silence, the congregation crowded behind him really felt that he was taking their lives, their worries, their ambitions, their sins and their sorrow for sin, all the spotted reality of their human nature, with its heroisms, its groping, its cowardices, and was lifting them up to God in hands that are shadowed with Christ's wounds. It was a mighty moment for any man whose name was in the heart or on the lips of Padre Pio.

I have been told of some marvels that have occurred at that moment, when Padre Pio prayed for someone who had not communicated with him in any way. Thus, for example, there was the lady who approached him after Mass with a request that he should pray for a matter that was vital to her. Before she could do so, he greeted her with the news that he had already prayed during the Mass at which she had assisted, told her what her intention was, and assured her that all would be well. Other examples of this can be found in the books published on Padre Pio.

A similar pause came at the memento of the dead, when Padre Pio's hands of prayer reached mercifully and longingly towards purgatory. I have been told that, on one occasion, a peasant whose son had just died, came running towards San Giovanni Rotondo, and shouted as she passed to some workers in the fields: "My poor Francesco is dead! But Padre Pio will put his hands into the flames and he will be safe!"

This was the feeling of every person who had the good fortune to commend some dear deceased one to Padre Pio: he would reach hands of prayer towards purgatory for him, and everything would be all right.

The greatest silence of all descended on Padre Pio at the priest's Communion; it was a silence that seemed to deepen itself in the breath of the Holy Spirit, until it became one with the abysmal silence of the Eucharist.

And what of the congregation during those periods of silence? The general impression one got from talking with these pilgrims and from reading the accounts they gave us, is that time seemed to be mysteriously swallowed up in that silence so that they were not conscious of any tedium. They were caught up in something bigger than themselves, they were lifting the veil to get a glimpse of a beauty that made the dry places of sorrow and suffering blossom again for them.

They had come, perhaps, with a November greyness in their souls, with that bitterness on the lips that disillusionment and vanished dreams so often leave; or perhaps it was simply that the slow grind of life, the incessant worry of providing for children, the thousand hidden heartbreaks that are never chronicled, had taken their toll; and, at the feet of Padre Pio they found joy and a great peace.

They remained kneeling long after the Mass had finished, as though they were loath to turn away from this vision splendid to where the heaped-up cares were waiting for them. And one feels that when they did turn away, it was to look on those cares with new eyes, because the after-image of that splendor would long be with them.

Some who came completely under the spell of Padre Pio remained permanently there. One of them is reported to have said: "I came here casually, and found for the first time that life has meaning. Paris, New York, London . . . you can have them all as far as I am concerned, for they are simply heaps of meaninglessness. I have found *meaning* here. And a man should stay, if he can, where the pieces of the jigsaw puzzle of life fit together and make sense. That is what San Giovanni is for me, and that is what kneeling daily at Padre Pio's feet means to me!"

The great things in life are paid for with pain. Turn to the story of any of the great founders or foundresses who have given splendid religious congregations to the Church, and you will find that the debt was paid by them. When Christ calls a soul to a special vocation, He marks that soul with the seal of His elect — with the seal of pain. Padre Pio was privileged to be a living witness to the wounds of Christ, and he had a mighty vocation of mercy to his fellowmen in the wasteland of the twentieth century. To kneel at his Mass, was to get a glimpse of the pain at the heart of his ecstasy — the price he too was called upon to pay.

Perhaps it is safe to say that nowhere in our time was there another priest who celebrated Mass as though he were bearing his cross through every moment of it. He indeed bore witness to the Passion of Christ in his body. There was an expression of suffering on his face at the supreme moments of the Mass, and his body was sometimes seen to twitch with pain. There were moments when he seemed lost in colloquy with God, when he moved his head as though nodding assent and he spoke some abrupt words. And there were those hands exposed only in the Mass, and otherwise hidden by the brown woollen mittens he constantly wore. Those hands could be seen, with the brown marks on them, the mystic shadow of the nails. And sometimes they bled. (Cf. Delfino Sessa, De Rossi, Parente, Carty, and others.)

The effect of all this on those who assisted at his Mass cannot be described. It searched the depths in every man; it descended like the angel to move the waters, to stir the stagnant places of the soul; it called to all the potential heroism in every heart, and spoke the eternal challenge of Calvary. When the Mass ended, every man saw a hand raised in blessing over him — a hand marked with a wound. Calvary became a reality, and the Mass appeared in all its shattering wonder for each and all. It is impossible to do more than reach vague groping questionings towards that silence of Padre Pio as he stood transfixed on the altar. That silence keeps its secret. But of one thing we can be certain — that this silence reached out to the silence in the heart of each one kneeling there, and according to the depth of spiritual silence within each heart the real message of Padre Pio was felt.

The great, radiating meaning in the life of Padre Pio was his Mass. We are living in a confused and bewildered world, a dry world, a world which becomes daily faster and faster, but gets nowhere and succeeds only in increasing its arid despair. Its social ideal is what Kierkegaard called "glittering inactivity"; it founders in spiritual bankruptcy, and the air is heavy with nihilism, with "angst," with despair. Such is the picture where religion has become a creed outworn. But sadder still is the picture which a book like Boulard's *Problèmes Missionaires de la France Rurale* gives us of what is happening within our own Catholic family.

Spiritual paralysis seems to have crept on the people. "Scarcely one man, at least among the natives of the place," reads one of the reports concerning a country parish, "any longer goes to Mass or fulfills his Easter duty. The great majority of the faithful are women. Religion is regarded as the affair of women and children, even though nearly all the inhabitants have been baptized and have received their first Communion . . . In a parish of 500 souls, only three women and some children attended Mass regularly. . . ." And is there not an Italian saying which defines a good Catholic as "a man whose wife goes to Mass every Sunday." It is against such a background that we must see the Mass of Padre Pio and realize what immense significance it has for our times.

Behind the wonder that was Padre Pio, there was a Divine Purpose, and that Purpose may well have found its supreme expression in the Mass of Padre Pio. We need a cosmic recall to the things of the spirit — and above all to the Mass, the pulsating heart of all Christianity.

May it not well be that Christ struck down Padre Pio and marked him with His Five Wounds, in order that he might stand at the altar as the living image of the Crucified, and that through him the Mass might become vital for us? For it is the Mass that matters, and until its power is again felt in the heart of our civilization, all will not be well.

7. THE WONDERS OF PADRE PIO

It is with the utmost caution that we approach the subject of the miraculous cures attributed to Padre Pio. The classic Catholic practice with regard to the miraculous is to sift the evidence so that every possible hint of a natural explanation is ruled out; for if a natural explanation so much as casts its shadow on the discussion, the miraculous is ruled out. Besides the sifting of the evidence, we seek for a divine purpose behind the miracle, for it would not be in harmony with the wisdom of God were He to interfere gratuitously and often with the working of a nature whose laws He has Himself ordained. The miracle is not even primarily a display of God's power for the sake of such display. As Monsignor Ronald Knox puts it:

"God does not do miracles *merely* to display His power, merely to show that He can do them. He does miracles, because He wants to draw our attention to this or that valuable movement among our fellow-men, to this or that sanctified career. What is more important than that we should take notice of a Saint? And who is more anxious that we shall take no notice of him, than the Saint himself? The very humility of the Saints would defeat God's purpose for them, if He did not take His own steps to shed lustre upon their self-effacing virtues. It is the miracle that gives us the assurance: 'Behold My servant, whom I have chosen' " (*Miracles* p. 10 C.T.S.).

51

There is another aspect of the alleged miraculous which must be taken into consideration. Unexplained and seemingly inexplicable phenomena are not *ipso facto* miraculous. There may be a fact waiting around the next corner of scientific progress which explains the present seeming miracle. Many years, for example, before penicillin was discovered, it was customary in parts of the Highlands of Scotland to rub mould from an old boot on a wound and utter a holy charm. The healing power was supposed to reside in the charm.

This somewhat homely example will serve to point the warning in Henri Bouillard's words: "The fact is that, even without being able to account for it clearly, the mind is aware, at least in a confused manner, that between unexplained phenomena and divine initiative, there is a qualitative jump, a passage from one order into another. It would be a fallacy to conclude to divine intervention from mere absence of scientific explanation. . . . A miracle is not simply a *prodigy* in nature; it is primarily a *sign* addressed to man, an evidence of the presence of the power of divine goodness. As such it belongs to the realm of religion. Divine initiative cannot be demonstrated scientifically. It is perceived in an act of religious consciousness" (See *New Problems in Medical Ethics* p. 249-250. Mercier Press).

The reader must bear with this preliminary caution which may seem as though we were stooping to shackle our feet before taking a step at all. It is better to grope one's way cautiously, with prudence checking our every step, than to rush forward with pious enthusiasm and ignore the presence of that "qualitative leap" altogether.

It would be easy to swell this chapter with reports of Padre Pio's alleged miracles taken from a hundred sources. It would be far from prudent to do so, for many of them would not survive elementary examination, much less the highly scientific investigation to which they should be subjected before the word "miraculous" can be predicated of them. There are considerations of the source of the evidence; of the possibility of a present or future explanation: and there are all those factors of what might be called the spiritual context of the alleged miracle. All of these have their pitfalls for the unwary.

We shall content ourselves, therefore, with isolating and examining one alleged miracle attributed to Padre Pio. It was reported by the *Corriere d'Informazione* of Milan on June 18th and 19th, 1947, with a typically frenzied journalistic heading. It is of special interest because it has a parallel in the famous Lourdes cure of Madame Biré, on August 5th, 1908.

The case concerned a young girl called Gemma di Giordi. From birth she was afflicted with double papillary atrophy, and according to the account given by her parish priest, was born without pupils. This darkness "amid the blaze of noon," these dark eyes in a world of beauty and color, present a very sad picture indeed.

It was just such a sight that puzzled the pharisees and led them to ask Christ whether such a catastrophe should be attributed to personal sin or inherited sin. Christ's answer was the glorious one, that this seeming cruel fate was for the glory of God.

It was also perhaps given to Gemma to bear her dark cross until the moment when it was lifted from her, that God might be glorified through his servant Padre Pio. Thus, in Monsignor Knox's words, this cure would become a pointing of God's finger to direct our attention to a "sanctified career" — to the place where Padre Pio was living quietly in the shadow of his self-effacing humility.

The first significant fact that emerges from the account is that Gemma's doctors — "Bonifacio, Cucco, and Contino, with other eye specialists" — considered it impossible that she should ever see. They looked on the possibility of such a cure as they would have regarded the proposition that one could cut with a knife without having a knife. It was as obvious as that. Gemma had no pupils: she would never see.

Her parish priest, Father Gambino, hints that her cure may well have begun through the intercession of St. Gemma Galgani to whom she was dedicated. The child improved slightly by the appearance of "a small opening in the eye through which, still without pupils, the child at the age of one was able to see her parents in a shadowy way when they came close to her."

Her eyes appeared as two black spots, incapable of movement, this immobility being painfully emphasized by frequent spasmodic convulsions of the eyelids. A heavy doom seemed to have been pronounced over this child, for whom the world was a place of shadows, colorless, and joyless. Science had spoken its final word and had no more to say.

But hope sprang eternal in the hearts of her parents, especially in the heart of her grandmother — one of those women in whom the faith of an earlier age still lived. She knew of Padre Pio; she had faith in him; she turned to him. She set off with the child on the long, tedious journey to San Giovanni, as one sets out in quest of one's last hope.

They assisted together at the Mass of Padre Pio. After the Mass, Padre Pio turned to the kneeling people and called sweetly: "Gemma, come here." Her grandmother led her forward to him, through the crowd who were now watching her with keen interest.

At that time she was seven years old. "You want to make your first Communion, isn't that so, Gemma?" he asked. He heard her confession and she had the privilege of receiving her first Communion from a hand shadowed by the wound in the Sacred Hand.

Nothing was said of her blindness, and no request for a miracle was made. Padre Pio simply blessed her with the words: "May our Lady bless you, Gemma. Be a good girl." A moment later the child cried out that she could see.

Reality came clamoring about her, and she looked at everything with fresh excited eyes. And the first human face the child saw was the kind and smiling face of the priest who was instrumental in curing her — a face radiant with joy.

Some months later, an eye specialist in Perugia, Doctor Caramaza, is said to have testified that Gemma could still see, but that she was still without pupils. "After a detailed examination," writes Father Carty (*op. cit.,* p. 97), "he confessed the continued and permanent intervention of the supernatural, because, without pupils, it is naturally impossible that the child sees."

There seems to be strong evidence for this wonder, and one may accept it as a genuine pointer to the sanctity of Padre Pio. Assuming that all the evidence put forward is correct — and there seems no reason for not doing so — we are up against something which science has no hesitation in declaring impossible. Given the whole background and character of Padre Pio, we have little hesitation in making the "qualitative jump" and concluding to "divine initiative."

It is interesting to set beside this case of Gemma di Giordi, the case of Madame Biré. After the death of two of her children in 1904, her health began to deteriorate. Violent headaches and porraceous vomitings brought on a coma, and when she recovered from it "she was found to be completely blind and to have lost the pupillary reflexes to light." This occurred in February 1908.

In August of the same year, she went to Lourdes, where she received Holy Communion at the Grotto. The priest, who was carrying the Blessed Sacrament back to the Rosary Church, passed by her. As he did so, Madame Biré, completely blind for five months, suddenly saw the statue of the Blessed Mother.

It was fitting that the first thing she saw should have been the image of her through whom she had received her cure, just as the first image to register in the quickened eyes of little Gemma had been the face of her kind benefactor.

Madame Biré was taken to the Medical Bureau, where the medical examination showed that against all scientific evidence to the contrary, she could read "the smallest print of a news-paper." A canonical enquiry was ordered by Msgr. Catteau, Bishop of Lucon, and its report, dated November 23rd, 1909, confirmed the findings of the Bureau.

A Belgian oculist examined her to discover if she was still able to see "with dead eyes." The phrase is a quaint and arresting one; it underlines the wonder of Madame Biré's cure as no amount of comment could do. He discovered that the phenomenon no longer existed. "The traces of papillary atrophy have disappeared. The lesions no longer exist and the cure is complete." Thus Madame Biré had been instantaneously cured at Lourdes of incurable blindness due to double papillary atrophy.

As far as we know, the case of Gemma di Giordi has not been submitted to such stringent examination. Nevertheless it has been pretty adequately documented, and we feel that it would stand up to any such examination. Thus, in the cure of little Gemma, we have an echo of a famous Lourdes cure. It is pleasing to find the name of Lourdes linked with that of San Giovanni Rotondo in two such similar wonders of mercy.

A whole list could be given of other wonders which have been alleged of Padre Pio. It would be a waste of time to do so — they cannot be established, and certainly those who aim at edifying us with their recital are not sufficiently concerned with producing proofs which would pass all of the seven rigid tests laid down by Pope Benedict XIV.

Thus, for example, Father Carty devotes several pages to the case of another cure due to an operation undergone at the advice of Padre Pio and about which the physician was gravely pessimistic as to the result. The subsequent cure *might* have been due in some way to Padre Pio, but might have been equally the result of the physician's skill. There does not seem to be much point in giving attention to such matters, especially under a chapter-heading which leads one to expect accounts of the miraculous.

Such an alleged miraculous cure falls down before the third of Pope Benedict's seven tests: "That if treatment has been applied, it is tolerably certain that it has contributed in no way to the cure." In the case cited, it is quite otherwise than "tolerably certain." In fairness to Father Carty, it must be added that he admits the inherent weakness in the case: "This beautiful and portentous cure is badly adapted to prove the supernatural in

Padre Pio . . ." but the word *beautiful* and the rather mystifying word *portentous* (with its suggestion of a portent, a prodigy), almost undo this admission. It is disappointing to find in a reputable writer this anxiety to force the issue at all costs.

One final aside. In dealing with the supernatural, it is sometimes unfortunate that the writer takes up a sort of theological or hagiographical superiority to the scientist, and treats the latter's stubborn entrenchment in the laws of nature as the obstinacy of a wilful child who just refuses to be told.

This attitude used to be much more frequent than it is today, for we have learned to listen to the scientist a lot more than we used to. The attitude does crop up, and shows itself sometimes in a single word. " 'The child is without pupils, it cannot see,' still blurts science . . ." reads Father Carty's enthusiastic account. Science does not *blurt* anything; it gives a calm and reasoned account of physical phenomena, and glorifies God by doing so.

I cannot pass over in silence the cures of the type of the Rosetta Polo Riva case as reported by Father Carty. The girl — a sufferer from acute endocarditis — is said to have had a vision of Padre Pio. His approach was heralded by a number of small white clouds which came together to form one cloud, and then "opened up and she saw the figure of Padre Pio as a half bust."

His second visit was heralded by a distant song which gradually became more distinct, and finally revealed itself as "a chorus of angelic voices that melted her heart and filled her eyes with tears." The culmination of this was "a great white cloud surrounded by the little heads of little angels." When this cloud opened "there appeared the Madonna with a marvelous face under chestnut hair and so resplendent with light that the child could not fix her eyes on her. . . ."

So far Father Carty . . . and at this stage we pause for breath, rub our eyes, and wonder. If the vision was so resplendent that the girl could not fix her eyes on it, how could she know the color of the Vision's hair — not to speak of the *red* dress and the *"blue* mantle embroidered with *gold* stars," and "the Child Jesus, with *blond* hair, wrapped in *rose-colored* swaddling clothes. . . ."

Now, this is really too much! The girl was twelve years old, an age at which young girls easily see visions and young maids easily dream dreams. Her "vision" — which, on the available evidence, is far from convincing — was a typical projection of adolescence, more than likely — as fine a piece of adolescent confection as one could wish.

It has all the elements of those Italian holy pictures which make one feel so acutely uncomfortable: the cloud, the heads of angels, the technicolor which may perhaps have been helped from a less spiritual source than the holy picture, the photos of the babies he had cured which Padre Pio (or rather his vision) showed her.

One would like to know more about Rosetta, and have a reputable Christian psychiatrist's report on her. Also, it would be interesting to know what reading the girl had been doing, or what was being read to her. Her vision ineluctably suggests a pastiche of pious confections representing the visions of the Sacred Heart, of Lourdes, of St. Anthony of Padua, the color-scheme being chosen in a typically adolescent fashion.

Another false note is struck by these words in the account: "Then he took off a glove and showed her his lacerated hand which was bleeding." Is it not strange that Padre Pio, a man of deep spiritual reticence who exposed his hands to the camera only under obedience, should be so demonstrative in vision? From start to finish, it all rings untrue.

It may seem unnecessary to break this butterfly of piety on the wheel — but it is not so. Such stories are in the honorable tradition of the acts of the martyrs and the golden legends of the Middle Ages. "These texts," remarks Bouillard with great wisdom, "are animated with such religious vitality that we find them of interest, even when we have become aware of their partly legendary character." But it is quite another matter when we are seriously asked to give credence to, and be edified by, a piece of pious gossamer spun by busy adolescent piety.

I wonder what Padre Pio himself would have had to say about

all this? Apparently he would have had nothing at all to say, for according to the girl's own account, he said to her in vision: "I cannot remember everything because I have so many, but you yourself must remember all your life what you have seen tonight."

To what does that "so many" refer? Am I to understand by it that Padre Pio was appearing so often, and in such extraordinary circumstances as the herald of our Lady, that he could not distinguish one occasion from another? Above all, was the girl warning me in advance not to check on the matter with Padre Pio himself — were I in a position to do so — because I would get no satisfaction? The first is, to say the least of it, improbable; and the second is, to say the least of it, naive.

But we have strayed into a rather squelchy pious morass, and we must hasten to get back to the less emotional and really edifying aspects of our subject.

8. PADRE PIO THE CONFESSOR

"The confessional is a stage shrouded in sombre curtains of tragedy, with one divine spotlight. . . ." From the height of the pulpit, the priest speaks to his assembled flock; but in the confessional he puts all the wonder of his priestly power at the disposal of each soul individually. Within the circle of that invisible "divine spotlight" are two people — one whose mighty privilege it is to take the place of Christ even to the extent of saying "I absolve you"; and the other who comes to lay before Christ the sad record of human weakness.

The secret of a great confessor is, of course, his own personal holiness, which the penitent knows as the sincere, humble, undivided attention given to him, and the great warmth of personal concern which meets him when he kneels at the confessor's feet.

Padre Pio did not preach; he did not correspond with outsiders; his whole mission was focused on the confessional. And he fulfilled that mission in a manner which was more wonderful than any of the wonders told of him.

According to Piera Sessa, Padre Pio wished people to look on him exclusively as a confessor. The great master work of his life was, therefore, his administration of the sacrament of penance. If we wish to see the great spiritual power of Padre Pio in all its splendor, in all its intense devotion, its superhuman endurance, we must look to his confessional.

61

The work of the confessional is, humanly speaking, the hardest and driest function of the priest. It is shot through with the realization of the mighty spiritual reality which vivifies it, and as such, a good priest regards it as among his most precious privileges. But any priest will acknowledge how much it takes out of him, when the sessions of confession are long, when the atmosphere becomes heavy, and when the effort of fixing one's attention becomes harder and harder.

It is said that only an artist, however imperfect he may be at his art, can really appreciate the masterpieces of that art by others. Perhaps only priests can really appreciate how magnificently, and with what giant spiritual endurance, Padre Pio devoted himself to the work of the confessional. I have heard more than one priest who had continued contact with Padre Pio, compare him with the Curé of Ars in this respect, than which a more splendid tribute could hardly be paid.

When his thanksgiving after Mass was completed, Padre Pio drank a glass of water — his sole breakfast — and then commenced the hearing of confessions. As is the Italian custom, he heard the confessions of men in the sacristy without a confession box or screen, and the confessions of women in the confessional.

It is a comment on the zeal and enthusiasm with which women flocked to him — and perhaps also a human comment on how the women who come to confess are the same who go to the sales — that the Capuchins had to put an iron barrier around the women's confessional. There was a time when enthusiasm outran due reverence; and in time a very wise plan was put in operation by which every penitent had to procure a numbered ticket on the previous day.

I have before me as I write, an admonitory leaflet, another evidence of the sane practical wisdom of San Giovanni, which warns the penitent that if he or she has come for a chat with Padre Pio, he or she had better dismiss the idea, because he is there to hear *confessions*. These practical steps precluded the possibility of a recurrence of that scene when the confessional crowd got so much out of hand that it was found necessary to call in the police to see that things were done in the tranquility of order.

This may perhaps shock our sedate, northern sense of spiritual decorum; but perhaps it is not to our credit altogether that we are incapable of such enthusiasm. After all, it is not a bad symptom for the regeneration of the world when we can call on the arm of the civil law to keep order among those clamoring to lay down their burden of sin. The new order of things at San Giovanni was, of course, much to be preferred.

His confessions continued until noon, when he took his one and only meal of the day; it consisted chiefly of vegetables, and was rarely supplemented with meat or eggs.

Dr. Festa, whose name has been mentioned earlier in connection with the medical examinations, made repeated visits to the friary and has told us that the amount of nourishment he took was very small. Only in the hot season did he have half a glass of beer with his meal, or water with some black coffee in it. Dr. Parente tells us that later the beer was replaced by lemonade.

A glass of water after Mass, a small meal at noon, and that constantly heavy program day after day: it is all certainly amazing! After dinner, he spent some time in recreation with the other members of the community, and then returned to his confessions and remained as long as there was a soul who needed him.

Wonderful tales are told of his gift for reading souls in the confessional. Considering the immense devotion which Padre Pio brought to the sacred tribunal, it is not at all surprising that he should have received such graces of wisdom and of insight.

One must be on guard, however, against the perennial human tendency to "cap" a story with a better one, a process which generally involves some embroidering of fact. We have many accounts, however, the sincerity of which can scarcely be doubted, and from which we can build a fairly complete picture of Padre Pio the confessor.

When a penitent came to him, his first searching glance was a kind of spiritual X-ray, which sometimes revealed the canker of insincerity by showing the hidden sins kept back, the twisted reasoning which covered with plausibilities of vanity and human respect things which should have been confessed sincerely and humbly. When this was so, Padre Pio immediately dismissed the penitent to prepare himself or herself with greater humility. At times, he did so quite sternly.

When such as these returned to him, however, they found another Padre Pio, a priest who knew their new-found sincerity and whose heart was open to them. There was nothing which froze the genial current of Padre Pio's warm humanity and deep spirituality, except this insincerity. He had warm sympathy for our weaknesses and for all the sad story of our stupidities when they were brought to him, or rather to Christ in his person, with humble repentance. Apart from the cases of insincerity and hypocrisy, Padre Pio came to crack the whip most often in the direction of gossip-mongering and scandal-peddling.

Here again, where a great grace — the gift of discernment of spirits — is found, we look for the cross, for it seems as an edict in spiritual destiny that this should always be so. It appears that the sins of his penitents caused intense pain to Padre Pio, and this may well be because he shouldered the guilt of so many and took their sins upon him.

This is a quality which Padre Pio shared with all the great confessors of all times: he did not listen like an impersonal judge to the sins told to him, but suffered a personal grief for each of them — a grief which was at once an act of reparation, and a shadow of that mighty sorrow in the Garden when the bitter chalice of human infidelities was offered to the lips of his Master.

While we are not inclined to accept literally the statements of those who say "that they have seen drops of blood on his forehead" (Father Carty: *op. cit.,* p. 20), we would subscribe wholeheartedly to the reality behind such an idea. For it testifies to the fact that every great confessor strives to "take our sins on himself" after the example of his Master, Christ.

Perhaps it was the sharing of their burden with his penitents, as well as the deepening of his own spiritual life, which kept Padre Pio on his knees before the Blessed Sacrament so late into the night. His concern for his penitents did not end with the absolution given to him; but his mercy and his compassion reached out to them that they might be given the grace to stand upright before God and to walk in His ways.

The great central light in the ministry of this *sacerdos magnus,* was the sacrament of penance, and we will not be wrong in viewing all the other aspects of his life in relation to it, for was not this what he himself implied when he said he wished to be regarded as a confessor? This must indeed be so, just as the centre of radiating charity in his life must surely have been daily intimate and often ecstatic contact with the Eucharistic Christ in the Mass.

The wonder of Padre Pio as a mighty confessor eclipsed all the phenomenal wonders told of him. As year followed year, he obtained his own wish more and more. The multitude came to him as to a great *confessor.*

9. PADRE PIO HIMSELF

"Look: I'll tell you what a Christian people is by the opposite. The opposite of a Christian people is a people grown sad and old. . . ." So, once again, Bernanos' M. le Curé de Torcy.

Christianity means joy, joy even in the midst of pain, it means the gift of eyes that see the rim of eternal hope on the edge of the world, the eternal hills beckoning across the valley of tears. Holiness is a cleansing of spiritual vision, and with that cleansing comes joy.

The greatest, the deepest joy of all, therefore, is in the heart of the saint. Was it not St. Francis de Sales, that glorious "personal columnist" among the saints, who said that a sad saint was but a poor saint. When we attribute holiness to a man, therefore, we look for joy; and when we find a sense of humor as well, we rejoice in the fact that our man of God is genuinely human too.

If it were possible to paint a grey "holy" picture of Padre Pio, one dare not put as frontispiece those laughing pictures of him as he stood in the garden among his fellow-religious, or those which show him chuckling over some petitions worded, perhaps, in a humorous way by people who knew that they did not need to be solemn towards Padre Pio.

It has been suggested by several writers that his joviality with visitors was a ruse to keep their minds on ordinary aspects of him. It is easy to understand how quickly a mawkish atmosphere could be created in such a situation, and how a man of sense like Padre Pio would take steps to avoid it.

I remember hearing of a monk in Mount Melleray, Ireland, who was being treated by a visitor, much against his manly grain, to some well-meaning piosities about the lovely sacrifice he was making, and who said abruptly: "Aye, surely, won't I get a terrific let-down if there is nothing at the end of it all!"

Padre Pio's humor could be salutary, too, especially when he met with pretentious humbug on the one hand, and exaggerated piety on the other. The Italian professor who handed in questions in Latin was told with a laugh that Italian was spoken here, and sent off to learn a little humility; and the monk who voiced his belief that he could become a saint by saying all his prayers aloud, was told to keep to a whisper or he would be taken for a simpleton.

The most delightful of all his sallies was, I think, his answer to a person who wanted to know why he chose the Capuchin Order from all the orders in the Church — whose number, as the ecclesiastical quip has it, only God Himself knows! Now, I have recently seen some accounts by various hands of why the writers became religious, and some of them are of a nature to make one vaguely uncomfortable. How refreshing is Padre Pio's answer! "Because I liked the beards the friars wear!" We have already referred to this, but it is worth recalling here in its context. (*Vide* Carty: *op. cit.,* pp. 61-63).

In every walk of life, but particularly among those who are gifted artistically in some way, one finds affected people who have spun about them a cocoon of egoism in which they live and move and have their somewhat futile being. It would be a mistake to think of Padre Pio as one who walked in the halo of his own wonder, as one who had in the faintest degree the least spiritual affectation.

Sometimes writers invite us to watch him "in spiritual action," so to speak, almost as though it were a "take" on a film set; thus, one writer rather inelegantly invites us to "imagine Padre Pio, all sweat and out of breath, raising himself in the air, and flying over the heads of the congregation. . . ." The absence of evidence does indeed leave one *imagining* it, and strengthens one's conviction that it is of much more spiritual use to see him with his two feet firmly planted on mother earth, carrying out his ordinary duties as a Capuchin with the utmost exactitude.

He was a simple, straightforward man, about whom a garment of what must surely be nine parts legend has been piously flung. He was not dwarfed by the legend; when one searches for the real Padre Pio, he emerges as bigger than any legend, since the confessional and the dispensation of the Mercy of Christ are bigger than all man's imaginings.

"Nothing could be further from hysteria," wrote Michael Hollings, "than this humble friar's behavior. For naturalness and humility work together in him. Whether he is taking snuff, ordering the women to stop gossiping in church, or joking with the community, there is nothing affected. You have only to see him to grasp his deep humility. It is difficult to explain; it has to be experienced" (*Life of the Spirit*: June, 1952). This is a fine tribute to the real greatness of Padre Pio, without which the alleged wonders would have as much spiritual significance as a conjuror's sleight of hand.

Humility is the bedrock of the whole spiritual edifice, and simplicity is its crown and glory. Perfection implies simplicity, for perfection is achieved through the great simplifying power of grace. It was this simplicity — as indefinable as the odor of a rose, but as immediately perceptible — that impressed one most in Padre Pio. There was something fresh about it, with that eternal freshness which goes with Christian perfection and the vivid realization of kinship with Christ.

Padre Pio was not permitted to preach, and his absence from the pulpit served only to underline the fact that he was himself a living sermon. No amount of eloquence could better the impression he made, the manner in which he stirred, by his very presence, the depths in those who came to him.

A valuable way in which we can get to the very essence of a man is through his writings — and especially through his letters. A man will reveal himself in a letter, where he might elsewhere be on his guard; for there is something symbolical of intimacy in the sealing of a letter by the sender and the breaking of the seal by the recipient alone.

There was a time when Padre Pio wrote letters to outsiders — even directed souls by means of letters; then for a time, he was forbidden to do so and outsiders were forbidden to write to him; later this ban did not hold for outsiders, but Padre Pio still considered himself bound by it.

We are indebted to Doctor Parente for having collected together some extracts from his letters, and it is of interest to examine them. One senses immediately his thirst for souls — that *Da mihi animas* of the real priest. "Do not worry about taking up my time," he assures a correspondent, "because we cannot spend our time better than in leading souls to sanctity."

Together with this thirst for souls, one finds also that tremendous sense of his own unworthiness and sinfulness expressed in words which seem utterly exaggerated, until it is remembered that this is how holiness speaks of sin.

When a St. Philip Neri or a St. Teresa claims to be the greatest sinner in the world, we are left very bewildered and wondering where we come in! But a St. Philip or a St. Teresa really *means* this, for they view every fault of theirs in the light of the unfathomable purity of God, and they measure every fault against the immensity of the graces given to them.

It is a question of spiritual sensitivity, and it might perhaps be illustrated by the something amounting to agony which a good musician can experience on hearing a magnificent symphony badly rendered, while the less sensitive ear hears it unmoved.

Nay more — the saint feels intensely that his own faults are those discords in the symphony of God, of Grace, of human destiny, and he suffers intensely because he knows intensely what he has marred.

It is with such considerations as these that we come to realize how sincere a man like Padre Pio can be when he writes: "In this I have been far worse than Lucifer. I know well that nobody is spotless before the Lord, but my own uncleanness is without parallel. Such is the deformity of my soul that when I think of it, my sacred habit seems to be horrified at my filth. . . ." Knowing the utter simplicity of the man, we may well regard this as having the authentic ring of holy sentiments profoundly felt.

His advice is characterized by a largeness of vision and good spiritual commonsense. "Walk with simplicity in the way of the Lord and do not torment your spirit," he writes to an over-anxious soul. "Learn to hate your faults, but to hate them calmly. . . . And if the devil makes a great deal of noise about you, rejoice, for this is a good sign. What we must dread is his peace and harmony with the human soul. . . ."

One does not look for literary qualities in the writing of Padre Pio, and it is therefore with a surprised pleasure that one comes on sentences as neatly phrased as Francis de Sales himself could have shaped them.

Thus, to some nuns who were bearing the cross of spiritual aridity: "The darkness that sometimes covers the sky of your soul is nothing but light. You imagine yourselves to be in the dark, and you are in the midst of the burning bush. As a matter of fact, whenever the bush is afire the surrounding air is darkened by smoke. The frightened spirit is then afraid of not being able to see or to understand anything any more. But it is exactly then that God speaks, and that He is present in the soul which listens, understands, loves, and trembles. . . ." And again: "Temptations, discouragement, disquietude, etc. are all merchandise offered by the devil, but rejected; therefore no harm in all this."

It is worthy of note that when a sentence of Padre Pio sockets itself in our memory, it is most often concerned with sorrow, with temptation, with spiritual darkness, with the cross. Thus: "The most beautiful *Credo* is the one we pronounce in our hour of darkness. . . ." "The life of a Christian is nothing but a constant struggle against itself, and its beauty does not become manifest except at the price of suffering. . . ."

Here we have the same qualities which made the spiritual advice of Padre Pio in the confessional so full of power. Those who watched him from a distance as he heard confessions in the sacristy, will remember that earnest gesture of his as he leaned toward his penitent, and as they read these extracts from his letters, they will remember that gesture. For they are the words of one who in every fibre of his being was a fisher of men.

What a magnificent spiritual director Padre Pio was! Look at this, for instance: "The sacred gift of prayer, my good daughter, is in the right hand of the Savior, and He will begin to give it to you in the same measure in which you become free and empty of self . . . and in the measure that you become well-grounded in humility. . . ."

Then there are those vivid phrases spun with the warp and woof of everyday things, and in the direct tradition of those images of the lilies, the lost coin, the shepherd and the sheep, which make the language of Christ so full of power.

"If you succeed in overcoming a temptation," he writes, "this will have the same effect on your soul as lye has upon dirty linen. . . ."

And again: "The devil has only one door by which to enter our soul — our will. There are no secret doors. . . ."

"Did you ever notice a field of wheat at harvest-time? Some ears stand up above others that are bent. If you take the former in your hand, you will find that they are empty; the others, the humbler ones, are full of ripe grain. From this you will learn that vanity means emptiness. . . ."

Notice, too, how with Padre Pio, a piece of Scholastic terminology can come to life with the addition of a metaphor: "Love tends towards its object, and it is blind in its advance. It does not see; holy fear illumines love."

And how St. Thomas Aquinas would applaud the terseness of such phrasing as: "Love and fear must always be together. Fear without love becomes cowardice. Love without fear becomes presumption. . . ." It has the authentic ring of a sentence from the *Summa*; it is a whole treatise in brief on that fundamental truth — that the Christian life is fear that loves and love that fears.

The photos of Padre Pio speak for themselves. His is a serene face — one of those that witness to peace of soul; it is a sensitive face that speaks the tenderness and compassion of the man; it is also the strong face of a man who looks for sincerity. It is the face of a great confessor — a face you can look at and find mercy and compassion there. It is a face worthy of his great Father, St. Francis, who must surely have regarded this son of his with a special joy.

Padre Pio was first and foremost a religious and an excellent one. He lived in a friary, and that friary was not just something which existed for the convenience of pilgrims — it was not, as it were, the shrine of a stigmatic. The common life, the daily religious routine went on unaltered, and Padre Pio was part of it.

All that he did, was done in obedience to his superiors. When they commanded him to cease hearing confessions or to say his Mass in private with only a server, he did so immediately.

This is the acid test, and Padre Pio proved that there was no spiritual pride in him. Before all else, he was a *religious,* and his real sanctity lay not in his stigmatization nor in the wonders told of him, but in the fact that he was a *good religious.* These essentials cannot be too insistently emphasized.

We shall see in the following chapter how the simplicity and humility of Padre Pio shone forth in his obedience to the Church's commands during the time when his "case" was under discussion in Rome.

10. THE CHURCH AND PADRE PIO

Whenever a wonder is announced, the first on the scene is the press, hot on the trail of a "story." Padre Pio was "news" from time to time, and it is a tribute to the thoroughness with which the press "covered" his case that the *Daily Mail* (19th June, 1920 — Cf. Thurston, *op. cit.*, p. 95) discovered "markings on his hands, sandalled feet, and *head!*" It gave an amusing picture of crowds besieging "the young Franciscan," refusing to confess to any except to him or to receive Holy Communion from any other priest, "and in consequence the rest of the monastery is idle."

It would be a sad picture indeed of the monastery (which was really a friary) as the *Mail* would have us see it — all those unfortunate fellow-friars of Padre Pio twiddling their thumbs in spiritual redundancy, all on what we might somewhat irreverently call the spiritual dole!

As good measure, well-pressed down and flowing over, we are given a picture of a Roman Monsignor rushing "over hill and dale for three days and nights in a motor-car to seek to calm the devout of Foggia, speaking in the name of Pope Benedict."

It is of great interest in the story of Padre Pio to trace the ecclesiastical reaction to him and to the question of his stigmata. It is of the utmost importance to look to the Church for guidance in all such matters, for it is only in her judgment, and not in the white-heat statements of popular enthusiasm, clerical or lay, that cool reason can be found. In the question of stigmata, however, and other physical phenomena it is worth while pointing out again that the Church wisely has *nothing* to say categorically about their supernatural origin, as was clearly pointed out in the canonization of St. Gemma Galgani.

While it is impossible that we should be able to say that *Rome has spoken* with certainty in the case of Padre Pio, it is however of great value to notice the climate of opinion in Rome about him, and it is also of the utmost importance to notice his own reactions to any directives given to him by Rome, since they are conclusive in any opinion we may reach about him or about any man.

De Lamennais, a man who, after having been largely responsible for lifting the Church of France out of the mud, went down into the murky depths of his only spiritual pride because he lacked the humility and the spiritual balance and vision needed to accept the decisions of Rome.

It is the glory of Padre Pio that he accepted Rome's will for him without a murmur, and the will of the Church as expressed in his ecclesiastical superior.

At first, Padre Pio was *persona grata* at Rome, chiefly because Pope Benedict XV was an admirer of his. "Padre Pio," he is reported to have said, "is in truth one of those extraordinary men whom God, from time to time, sends on earth to convert mankind." This high personal opinion fixed opinion in favor of Padre Pio. The year was 1921, and matters remained thus for some years.

Came the year 1924, and a special number of *Vita et Pensiero* for the seventh centenary of St. Francis' stigmata. The Franciscan Rector of the Catholic University of Milan, the famous theologian Father Gemelli, claimed in his contribution to this number that only the stigmata of St. Francis and St. Catherine of Siena could be regarded as having a supernatural origin, all other cases being ascribable to some psychopathic condition or even to self-inflicted wounds.

This was a sweeping statement and a challenging one; its challenge was taken up by the Jesuit *Civiltà Catholica,* which censured it as "rash and inexact."

There the matter rested, but this quick crossing of theological swords on the matter was sufficient to create a current of caution in Rome. The previous year, indeed, a *non constare* had been issued from Rome to the effect that the phenomena of Padre Pio "could not be affirmed to be certainly supernatural."

In 1925, an "extraordinary commissary" was sent by the Holy Office to San Giovanni, and placed as superior over all the Capuchin houses in the province of Foggia.

In 1926 and in 1931, certain books on him were condemned, and there was a ban put on visits to him and on correspondence with him. He could say Mass, but only in private, and he was forbidden to hear confessions or to preach.

But Father Martindale, to whose article in *The Month* we are indebted for these details says that the new superior and commissary "soon became a defender of Padre Pio's virtues and great prerogatives.' " From that time onward, the official attitude to Padre Pio has gradually become more and more favorable.

This was seen, for example, in the manner in which the announcement of the 1952 ban on eight books concerning Padre Pio emphasized that no censure of the stigmatic himself was implied. Such care to distinguish between the person of Padre Pio and the indiscretions of his biographers is indicative of the esteem in which he was held.

What of Padre Pio himself during that period when, on account of Pope Pius XI's well-known caution about the preternatural, and the same Pope's great respect for Father Gemelli, a reaction of distrust in high places set in against Padre Pio? It was indeed a heavy cross for him. He saw a curtain of silence descend between him and the people whom he loved: the pulpit was forbidden to him, he could no longer hear confessions, he could no longer feel the warm reality of the people about him as he uttered the *Orate Fratres.*

Back in 1914, he had written of "these devout people who want me to remain among them at all costs. I don't just imagine that they do. No, they have shown it on various occasions, especially on my last return home. When I entered the town, they came out thanking the Lord and shouting *Evviva!* on account of my return. . . ."

There was a strong bond of union between Padre Pio and his people, as is witnessed by the great numbers of the ordinary Italian peasant folk who constantly came to him. And now, Rome had drawn a curtain between him and them, and had cut him off from what was the very heart of his ministry, from that to which he was so passionately devoted — the administering of Christ's mercy to souls through the sacrament of penance.

"I find only one gentle lament in a letter of Padre Pio's," writes Father Martindale, "about this restriction of his liberty of action, and the lack of moral support on the part of those who held for him the place of God. His obedience has always been perfect."

There is a hint here that his cross was of double weight, owing to the attitude of his own superiors. We have no further evidence to show what that attitude was; but it would be only natural, had it taken the form of a certain amount of annoyance at this turn of events. This kind of publicity is never welcome to a religious community, and if the reaction which seems to be hinted at in this extract did indeed exist, it was indeed regrettable but very natural indeed.

San Giovanni Rotondo became one of the pilgrim centres of the world. Scores of giant motor-buses arrived there bringing pilgrims from the U.S.A., from Australia, from Canada, from all over the world. There are thousands of testimonies from these pilgrims of the good they derived from their visit to this unpretentious place where they met with deep and unpretentious holiness.

As was inevitable, some came to scoff — and remained to pray, or departed silently with the problem of something that was not contained in their philosophy. The majority came with the weight of their sins and of a world perplexed and sad. At San Giovanni they met the freshness that blows from the fields of God, and they went back renewed in spirit.

A monument to the great practical charity of Padre Pio stands just above the friary: it is the *Casa Sollievo della Sofferanza,* a very fine, big hospital. It is the answer to those who look on the Christian mystic and the stigmatic as one who beats luminous wings in some sort of an unearthly garden of Eden all his own.

In 1940, as reported by Doctor Parente (*op. cit.,* p 123), Padre Pio said to some visitors: "Rising above selfishness, we must bow down to the suffering and the wounds of our fellow men. . . . In every sick man, it is Jesus in Person who is suffering; in every poor man, it is Jesus Himself who is languishing; in every man who is both sick and poor, Jesus is doubly visible. . . ."

This is the authentic voice of charity, and it is the doctrine of the cup of water splendidly interpreted. It reminds one of those words of that giant of charity, Father Etienne Pernet, founder of the Little Sisters of the Assumption: "In the person of the poor sick man on his miserable bed, see Christ the Divine Leper."

With such sentiments as these so clearly at heart, it was not surprising that Padre Pio should have been acutely aware of the need for a good hospital in that part of Italy. The thought was father to the deed, and he set about realizing it himself in what some men called "a mad and hair-brained scheme." We end this account of Padre Pio with some details of the courage and tenacity which brought about the realization of his dream for helping his fellow men.

It seems (see Parente: *op. cit.,* chap. 15) that Padre Pio first discussed the matter in 1940 with three people, anonymously referred to as "three shipwrecked souls." One of the characteristics that mark works which seem inspired by God is that they *do* seem crazy; as when founders lay down great schemes with no resources save their trust in God.

Padre Pio's scheme was nothing less than to build and equip a complete modern hospital at "some 2,400 feet above sea level, on a barren mountain slope, twenty-five miles away from Foggia, the nearest town of any importance." There was no railway; water and electricity would have to be brought in.

So Padre Pio faced his great scheme — with no resources except a piece of mountain, and a gold coin that someone had given him for charity. He presented this coin to "the three ship-wrecked souls" as the first contribution to the fund.

Small donations began to trickle in. A kiln was established and the job of digging out stone from the mountain began. Building machinery was got — and meantime the debt began to soar. However, an unexpected gift of one million three hundred thousand *lire* came unexpectedly to hand. But on June 10th, 1940, Mussolini let loose the dogs of war, and the whole undertaking had to be suspended.

Let it stand as an answer for ever to those who think of Christian mystics as essentially impractical, that it was Padre Pio who had the good sense to advise the investment of the funds in a landed estate. When the post-war lire fell to one eightieth of its pre-war value, the wisdom of this was seen.

Meantime, Padre Pio continued to nurse his project undaunted, in prayer and in sacrifice. By 1946, only four million *lire* were in hand — that is, only 50,000 *lire* in pre-war currency valuation. It was pitiably small, but the sponsors kept rigidly to their rule of not asking for aid but relying on the providence of God. This is the spiritual stamp of big men with spiritual vision.

In the autumn of 1947, that splendid Englishwoman, Barbara Ward, went to San Giovanni, and in consequence of that visit — for Barbara Ward has no half-measures about anything she sets her mind to — UNRRA assigned 250 million *lire* towards the new hospital.

This enabled the work to get really under way, and the hospital now stands — an absolutely magnificent structure — as a monument to a man whose intense love of God knew how to express itself in love and service of his neighbor.

Such, then, are the facts, and such is the man. Whatever may be the final decision on the phenomena and the wonders of Padre Pio, there is no disagreement on what is more essential than any phenomenon or any wonder. For all agree that he was a great priest.

Padre Pio died on September 23, 1968. Less than five years later, on January 16, 1973, the Most Reverend Valentino Vailati, Archbishop of Manfredonia (Foggia, Italy) delivered to the Sacred Congregation for the Causes of Saints in the Vatican all the documents required for the "Nihil Obstat" which would permit the official introduction of the cause of beatification and canonization of the Servant of God Padre Pio of Pietrelcina.

Included among these documents were: a copy of all the writings of Padre Pio, totalling twelve typewritten volumes; a complete critical biography of Padre Pio consisting of over 500 typewritten pages; and a collection of 575 articles on the chronology of Padre Pio's life, on his practice of all the virtues, on the extraordinary phenomena that occurred during his lifetime; and on his reputation for sanctity during life and after death.

If Padre Pio will be beatified and later canonized, it will surely be because he was a great priest and a faithful religious. Symbolic of this, perhaps, is the fact that at the moment of his death the wounds disappeared from his body.

II

MARTIN DE PORRES

1. UGLINESS IN THE EYES

Don Juan de Porres watched, with deep secret disgust, his wife Anna Velasquez tying a red bow on his daughter's hair. The bow seemed to blaze against the duskiness of the child's skin, and the hands that tied it were of the same dark velvety texture. He looked down at his own white manicured hands resting with languid grace on the deep folds of his scarlet cloak. The bow on the child's hair matched the redness of his cloak, and as he noted this, it suddenly became coldly and callously clear to Don Juan de Porres, soldier of Spain and aristocrat of Lima, that there was no other point of contact between him and his daughter than the color of the cloak and its echo in the bow.

His son, Martin, another black little horror, played quietly on the floor, and if his father looked at him at all, it was only to recoil from this visible evidence of his own bad taste. By what unaccountable lapse had he, Don Juan de Porres, allowed himself to be bewitched by blackness? In the opinion of Lima's perfumed and bejewelled society, Don Juan could not have behaved in a more eccentric fashion had he dressed himself in his gayest colors and then proceeded to roll himself with grand abandon in a heap of coal dust. When a black daughter and a black son were born to Don Juan, Lima society was amused and smiled over its wine. Don Juan knew they were smiling, and he found the weight of his crushed vanity unbearable.

85

He ceased to live with Anna, for his vanity could no longer endure the narrowness and meanness of the street called Espiritu Santo where he had made his home. Don Juan de Porres had risen in the ranks of the army and, which was of much greater moment, in the esteem of the king, so that, like many a petty soul in every age, he felt his home as clay clinging to his wings and hindering his flight into the perfumed reaches of the highest society in the land.

Don Juan suddenly decided, as he watched his wife giving a final part to the red bow, that he had had quite enough of all this, that he would shake the clay from his wings. Between him and the little black woman he called his wife, he sensed at that moment a pageant of all his lost opportunities in Lima society — opportunities of alliances with white beauty, with rank, with wealth. But a black blight had come on them all, through his own stupidity. . . . He muttered something about an engagement to keep, and left abruptly.

Anna lifted her arms from the tub into which she had just put her washing, and rested them on the edges. She was looking at the door that had just closed on her husband, and, with a woman's intuition, she knew that he was gone. She had no need to turn and see the little bag of gold on the table. She knew. She had known for a long time that she had become just a heap of clogging blackness in his life, a burden and a social disgrace. She was not left to guess at this, moreover, for he had taken many opportunities of telling her so with the utmost bluntness and brutality. And now, he was gone. . . .

The soap-suds dripping from her elbows were nice and white. Little Martin's eyes sparkled as he watched them gathering on the round, shiny elbows and dripping oozily to the ground. Fascinated, he toddled forward and held out his tongue to catch a drop. His mother saw him, and the whiteness of the suds seemed to mock her.

"Go along with you," she snapped, pushing him away, "if those suds could make you white, I would put you to bed in them.

But nothing can change you from a love-killing black horror, any more than it can change me. Go on," she added, pointing to Jane, "and take that with you too out of my sight."

Martin took his sister's hand and went out into the street. Young as he was, he knew all too well this mood of his mother's — the mood in which he was blamed for everything, and in which she had no kindness for him but only hard words about his blackness.

He held out his hands and looked ruefully at them. Then a gaily-colored carriage came rolling grandly along the street, and Jane and Martin forgot their sorrow in watching it. From the windows, white-skinned ladies and gentlemen looked out. They scarcely noticed the two black children, but little Martin noticed *them*.

Strong color-associations began to form themselves in his awakening brain: white — which stood for beauty, prosperity, and all the good things of life; black — which meant ugliness, poverty, and toil. But as year followed year and Martin grew in age and wisdom, no resentment towards the white rich had place in Martin's heart.

Very early in life he learned the lesson that all men are equal in the sight of God: a simple enough truth, but one which came to young Martin with the force of a revelation, and became at once the inspiration of and the key to his life.

Perhaps the first manifestation of this truth in the life of Martin was his attitude to the poor. He seemed utterly incapable of passing a poor person without giving what he possessed — even if it happened to be he money for a message on which he had just been sent. He had promised his mother that this would not occur, but in spite of that, the sight of poverty and suffering made him go back on his word, and face another thrashing from his mother when he returned home.

Charity, then, became for this child the strong temptation that led him astray. Happy indeed is he whose childhood vice is a ruling passion of charity. Francis of Assisi knew that passion, when he left his father's bales of cloth untended in the market-place, and ran after a beggar whom he thought he had slighted.

In the beginning, such acts, with Martin, were dictated simply by goodness of heart; but before long the beginning of a solid philosophy began to form behind them — the philosophy that all men are the brothers of Christ, sons of the Father, and if sons, heirs also, heirs indeed of God and joint heirs with Christ.

The life of St. Martin of Porres can be — and has been — written as a series of wonders, breath-taking in their simplicity, as fresh and refreshing as the dewy pearls on the hedgerows glistening in the morning sun. But let it be emphasized at the very outset of this little life, that miracles and wonders count for nothing except as fingers pointing to a greater wonder — the wonder of God's grace and charity in a human soul. In reading the lives of the sainly wonder-workers, therefore, the flash and glory of the wonders they work should not be allowed to dissipate our vision, but should focus it clearly on the greater wonder which gives meaning and cohesion to them all.

The centre of Martin's real life, then, is an intense realization of the brotherhood of men in Jesus Christ. At this early stage of his life, he may have expressed it simply to his sister Jane by the respect in his eyes for her God-given black beauty.

Meantime, we have left Anna Velasquez with her arms plunged in the suds of her washing. It is a safe guess that you would find her thus if you called at any time in the long years that followed her husband's decision to leave her. The little money she had was soon spent, and there was nothing for it but to take in washing and toil over it from morning till night.

At the end of a year she felt that every month of the twelve months just past was marked by a long line of soap suds — hour to hour, day to day, week to week, month to month linked by two black hands making a white line.

For a long time there was bitterness in her heart, and there is no bitterness like loving words gone sour in the soul. He had loved her, but fortune had smiled on him and he had become proud, despising her. Still, she loved him, for a woman's love can be deathless: and she hated her skin that had turned him from her.

When she looked at her children, she saw the same blackness. When the gloom was thickset on her soul, she saw little Martin and Jane as just part of it, and she found herself almost hating them because they were not as their father. But such feelings can be safely left to be conquered by a mother's love.

When a woman knows so poignantly where every coin comes from, it is hard not to be hedgehoggy when instead of a loaf the little son brings nothing but a charity done in the sight of the angels. It is very beautiful, but you cannot put it on a platter and slice it to feed three hungry people. Nevertheless, this very charity of his must have had a lot to do with reconciling her to her life and to her children, for it is of the essence of charity that it should begin at home (in every sense), and he is a poor saint who is an ogre in his own kitchen.

But such reconciliation was to come. For the moment, she thought how bitter it was to have a black skin. Yet, black or white, the children had to be fed and life must go on. The cycle seems ever the same — love, disappointment, hardness, bitterness, the softening of time, and the triumph of charity, with peace as its fruit. It was to be so with Anna Velasquez. Meantime, there was the bitter struggle that life might go on.

2. THE PROSPECT BRIGHTENS

God's weights and measures do not conform to any standard of earth, and therefore a feather of prayer or of charity may tilt the scales of grace much more than earthly wisdom would expect.

It seemed a small and insignificant thing that little Martin should slip a coin into a poor woman's hand, because he was sensitive to sorrow and suffering, but He who watched the act and knew its beauty was He who said that a cup of cold water given in His Name should not go without its reward. And, therefore, a certain measure of grace came to Don Juan de Porres, aristocrat and soldier of the king of Spain.

It came to him, unaccountably it seemed, as he moved in the fashionable society of Guayaquil, Equador, to the north of Peru. A man needs to be utterly depraved through every vestige of his being before his conscience becomes utterly paralyzed and dumb. As long as there remains any real good in a man, his conscience may raise its head at any moment and speak through the accumulated dust and cobwebs of neglect.

So Don Juan's conscience spoke to him, telling him that, despite his perfumes and his finery, he was but a poor specimen. There are times when the conscience can speak with the coolness of steel in every word, and this was one of them. Don Juan ordered a carriage for Lima.

The same Lima, the same narrow, dust-breathing street oddly called Espiritu Santo, the same . . . but surely those two little

91

ragged children were not his? Yet, how could they have been otherwise than ragged and ill-fed when their father thought more of his own social advancement than of his flesh and blood.

Poor Anna may very well have been slaving at her tub when that carriage drew up at the door. We can imagine her nervously drying her hands, and checking a hope half-born in her soul lest it should change to bitterness and stifle her. She moves diffidently to the door, watching him alight. But there is something in the way he sweeps into the little house which assures her, and she knows that he has returned — not, of course, to stay, for he has grown entirely out of her world, but to acknowledge that he has a duty towards her and to ease her intolerable burden. Full of joy she welcomes him and rushes to the door to call her children, who are peeping shyly at a father who is a stranger to them.

He steps forward and, putting his arms about them, draws them into the little kitchen. He fusses over them. What poor clothes they have — he must alter that. There wasn't a child in Espiritu Santo who could read or write — but his children would get the best of education that they might be fitted to take their place in the world. They were his children, and he would make them a credit to him. They were to come with him to Guayaquil to live with their uncle, Don Diego de Miranda, and be educated there. Anna would not want for money nor have to slave. . . .

For several weeks, Don Juan stayed with his family. There was scarcely another topic of conversation in the street called Espiritu Santo, and her neighbors began to have more respect for their washerwoman. What the ladies of Lima thought of it all just does not matter: for Don Juan was not in the least concerned.

We have all known the rich relation who hits the family like a breeze, scatters a bit of money for a day or two, promises the moon, and breezes off again to breeze elsewhere, leaving things even more sour than before. Don Juan was not one of these, for, when his time came to leave for Guayaquil, he had his little son and daughter with him — radiantly happy in their new clothes. Anna said good-bye to them with great joy in her heart, for they were to get an opportunity in life far beyond her fondest dreams.

Martin stood with his hand in his father's and watched the bustle and excitement of Callao harbor, where they were embarking for the north. Small groups of men met together and parted like eddies on the surface of a river; men bargained with men over their wares; little knots of people gathered around those who were departing; sailors climbed the masts to fix the sails.

But it was none of these that held the young boy's attention and saddened his joy. It was the endless stream of blacks going to and coming from the boat, their backs bent under heavy loads. What were these loads, he asked his father. Gold, he was answered, gold for the king's service. Martin said no more. In his heart of hearts, he knew that the real gold, to the eyes of the King of Heaven, was the poor black who toiled and perspired under a burden too heavy for him.

At Guayaquil, Don Diego de Miranda awaited them — an old man, with grey-white hair and a face like a blessing. The children liked him at once, but the old man's reaction was, at first, one of shock. He recovered quickly and chuckled with a kind of good-natured gobble in his beard. So Don Juan had chosen a negro beauty: well, well, we always were an original family. So he chuckled, and drew the two little ones to his side with a hug of welcome. They felt his kindness about them with the rough, snug warmth of a blanket.

Life was good at Guayaquil — a nice house, plenty to eat, a carefully-chosen tutor to teach them and, above all, an atmosphere of kindness in which the children opened like flowers in the sun. Martin learned quickly and settled to work with a simple eagerness which delighted all. Very soon his uncle realized that he was a lad of promise and he spared no pains to educate him. Jane was slower but very willing, and showed signs of developing into a fine woman.

So life went on for two happy years, until one morning the house was in great excitement because their father, Don Juan de

Porres had been appointed governor of Panama.

Two things seemed clear to Don Juan — that he must visit Lima before his departure, and that the society of Panama would not be impressed by their new governor's offspring. A governor with black children, just fancy, my dear!

So Don Juan had a solution. Don Diego liked the children very much, and had no hesitation in allowing Jane to live with him until such time as he should find a suitable husband for her.

Calling Martin to him, Don Juan told him that he must return to his mother in Lima and think about his future. Was there anything he would like very much to be? A trader, perhaps, or an accountant?

Little Martin — now a sturdy lad of ten — did not hesitate a second over his reply. He would like to be a doctor. This wish took his father by surprise and he laughed heartily. But Martin obviously meant what he said, and to his great joy, Don Juan gave a very warm consent. He knew the very man in Lima who would teach him. His name was Marcelo de Rivero. . . .

Martin did not return to his old home in Espiritu Santo, for his mother had gone to live with her friend Doña Francisca Velez Miquel near San Lazaro. It was a great joy to Anna to see her son again after two long years. She had heard great reports of him, of his goodness, his application, and his progress in study. Now he was coming home to prepare to be a doctor.

Anna was a little shy of this son of hers, for, young as he was, she felt there was quite a widening gap between them. She could not read or write, and here was her son, after two years' application, returning with what must have seemed to her a weight of learning. Would he be ashamed of her now, as his father had been? But one look at those simple, candid eyes and she knew her Martin was returning unspoilt.

It was necessary for his work that Martin should live near the little dispensary of Dr. de Rivero. He found lodgings with a lady called Ventura de Luna. Every morning he rose very early and attended Mass in San Lazaro before going to his work. At Mass and at work, nobody noticed him very much. He was just a negro boy who was there at Mass and there at the dispensary.

But Dr. de Rivero knew differently. Within a short time, there was not a bottle in his little store which Martin could not handle with skill. Then, as one of his biographers tells us, something happened which put his name on everyone's lips.

Dr. de Rivero had been called away and Martin stood by the window, mixing some medicine. Sounds of a fight and the patter of feet running excitedly down the street, filled the room. Distressed, Martin looked out, and what he saw galvanized him into action.

They were bringing a stabbed and bleeding Indian to the dispensary. He poured some water in a basin and unrolled some bandages. By this time, they had come in and there was a babble of excited voices around Martin, calling for Dr. de Rivero. They scarcely heeded the little black assistant, until he stunned them all by saying:

"Dr. de Rivero is away, so I must attend to the poor man myself."

Well, of all the presumption — this little black *was* getting beyond himself — and the people crowding the little room voiced their sentiments in no uncertain manner.

But something about the boy's movements silenced them, as they watched the sureness and speed with which he moved from bottle to bottle, mixing his salve; the competence with which he washed and dressed the wounds; the fading of the tortured pain from the man's face, and the relief which took its place, as much from the soothing words of the little negro as from the healing ointment he applied.

Martin worked away, altogether unconscious of the awed silence he had created around him. When he had finished, he looked up from his work and said simply: "He'll be all right now."

But the wonder of it all was carried from end to end of Lima. Anna Velasquez heard it, and felt very proud of her son. She saw a great career ahead for Martin.

3. A CHANGE OF PLANS

One day Martin asked his landlady for a candle. For some reason, the good lady had never thought of his needing one. He left the house in the early morning, worked all day long, and returned late at night. Ventura de Luna very naturally thought that the lad would be so anxious to get to bed as soon as possible that he would find any kind of light utterly superfluous.

But Martin had learned to love his little room and to value the privacy it gave him. This love of a room figures as a regular feature in the lives of the saints, for if there is anyone who is never less alone than when alone, it is the saint.

"Keep thy cell," advises the "Imitation of Christ": and the great French thinker, Pascal, said that "all the evil of the world comes from one single thing — that men do not know how to remain quietly in one room."

A room of one's own is essential to being alone: being alone is essential to converse with God: and converse with God is the seeding of sanctity.

Ventura de Luna soon began to notice, even very late at night, a ribbon of light showing under the door. She became curious — as landladies will in every age and clime — to the point of one night slipping quietly to the door and putting her eye to the keyhole.

What she saw amazed her. Martin knelt upright before the

rough crucifix that hung on the wall. There was a strange joy on his face and strange tears in his eyes. Ventura drew back in wonder and astonishment.

Well she might: for it is a wonderful thing to look on a face that is lifted up to the great Mysteries of the Incarnation and the Redemption, and suffused with their radiance.

Martin's face was lifted to his God. The joy in his face was the joy of sonship: the tears were for the sins of men, shadowing the agonizing Soul of Christ, just as the flickering candle was passing shadows over the crucifix before him.

Martin was not reading, as Ventura had expected. Or was he? . . . When St. Bonaventure asked St. Thomas Aquinas: "What is the secret of your learning? What is your book?" the great saint turned to a crucifix that stood between him and the light, and said, pointing reverently to it, the while his voice deepened like a bell with sincerity: "My secret? My book? Br. Bonaventure, see my book!"

Martin, too, seems to have learned to read in that book. To do so, one's soul must have learned to live in silence — in that silence wherein a man truly finds himself, and to which he owes all that is in him of depth and of good. Martin found that silence in his room, when the rustling sounds of the night faded to echoes of a forgotten world, and the air about him was alive with the rhythm of his prayer.

And one night, when the silence of his prayer was around him, Martin decided on a change of life. He felt that the Master was calling him in a special way to the feast, but he would be mindful of the injunction to "sit down in the lowest place." He would not aspire to the priesthood. He felt himself unworthy of being a lay brother. He would offer his services as a helper to the Lima Dominicans in Santo Domingo.

It was a shock and a disappointment to his mother, who had already dreamed herself ahead on a long road of success for her son. Now he was talking of turning his back on it all, and taking work as a menial servant. It is easy to sympathize with her, for she could not see the decision as part of a grace-filled horizon that held the eyes of her son and would not let him lower them.

As for Dr. Rivero, the news came to him as a great shock, and he did all in his power to dissuade Martin from his purpose. He pointed out to him the good he could do by remaining to heal the sick. But Martin only smiled and said he must go.

It was not easy for him to say good-bye to the kind-hearted doctor, to the little shop with its bottles and bandages, and to the three happy years he had spent there. But this decision had been taken, and the decisions of essentially simple natures are of great strength.

Martin's simple decision to work as a servant for the Dominicans was full of significance: it was the decision of a lad of fifteen to turn his back on the valley and face the heights.

But surely, it may be objected, he merely crossed his own doorstep in his own town. . . . There is a famous saying about the miraculous walking on the waters, that the distance did not matter since the wonder lay in the first step.

That Martin de Porres considered that step over his threshold a significant and irrevocable one, is seen by the care he took to take leave of all his friends before starting his new life. "It will not be the same now," he said simply, "for my time will not be my own."

What did the Dominican Fathers think of this little black who came, one morning, with great simple earnestness in his face, and asked to be taken into the monastery that he might be the servant of the fathers.

But they could not pay him anything, the prior explained, for they were poor and the monastery was already in debt. Martin explained that he was not interested in money, but only in the service of God.

Did he wish to become a lay brother then? the prior asked. No, the lad insisted, he wanted to be a servant — a servant of the lay brothers. It must have seemed a strange request to the good fathers, but, after some deliberation, they accepted him, to Martin's great joy.

The habit worn by priests and religious is a symbol, as is evident from the words used at a "clothing" ceremony, of the laying aside of the old man and the taking on of the new. "The habit does not make the monk," says Thomas à Kempis wisely: but it does stand for a change of life, for the lifting of the eyes to an ideal.

Martin, too, would have a "habit" to keep himself reminded that now he was to belong to Christ. He had a habit of white wool made, "somewhat on the style of that worn by the priests and lay brothers," but without the long scapular front and back. A large rosary hung about his neck and another from his leather belt. And so Martin began his new life.

"To every man," said the poet, "there openeth a way and ways — and a Way." . . . Martin's way was the lowliest of all. Clothed in the wedding garment, he went shyly into the supper-feast of the Lamb of God. But he sat down in the lowest place of all.

Immediately the Master of the feast saw him. He moved towards Martin, with the first words of His invitation already on His lips — "Friend, go up higher."

Today, a great devotion is springing up to St. Martin de Porres, and the headquarters of that devotion are in New York.

It is surely a wonderful thing, and a mighty proof of the exaltation of the lowly, that this poor black who came to a monastery three hundred years ago as a menial servant, should be rapidly engaging the attention of men in the most complicated, cross-purposed and sophisticated age in the world's history.

It is according to the wise dispositions of Providence that he should come to us as a challenge.

4. THE CHALLENGE OF SIMPLICITY

A challenge to what? . . . To our worship of the serpent of human wisdom and to the clay in our vision. For the keynote of the soul of Martin de Porres was a great simplicity — the simplicity that Christ had in mind when He said: "Unless you become as little children, you cannot enter into the Kingdom of Heaven."

The twentieth century has travelled so far into the waste-land of sophistication, that we have lost the idea of what simplicity means. To be childlike does not mean to be childish: the first is a virtue, the second a nuisance.

Simplicity, the virtue of being childlike, is a mighty power: it is that singleness of vision by whose presence the whole world becomes lightsome, and the absence of which means that the whole world becomes a darkness, a muddle, a distraction from God.

"If your eye is single," says Christ, "your whole body will be filled with light." Simplicity could be defined as the singleness of the spiritual eye. Such singleness is achieved by the great simplifying power of grace.

It might be possible to uphold the thesis that the virtue of simplicity finds a more congenial seeding-ground in the Black than in the White. His is a cultural heritage more in tune with nature, without the dryrot of centuries in it, and the mighty

101

simplicities of Christianity find a kindlier place in it than in the frost-hardened western soul.

To listen to a congregation of Blacks praying is to realize just how simply we can speak with God. To hear prayers spoken in such simplicity must surely make one think, with a certain homesickness, of the time when the dew was on these truths for western souls.

Martin de Porres is the saint of this simplicity: were he to come on earth today, he would find his closest kindred in those poor Blacks least affected by contemporary pseudo-sophistication.

We have lingered over this virtue of simplicity because it is so essential that we should bear it in mind in our approach to the life of St. Martin. It is the forest which we must not miss for the trees: and, as the "trees" here are scintillating wonders, dazzling in their simplicity, the task is not an easy one.

Martin de Porres was a delightful little man, who could amuse you spiritually by raising the dead at one moment and making (and keeping) an appointment with a rat in a cabbage garden at another.

To admire the wonders of the saints and to praise God for them is an excellent thing: but it can become unsanctified curiosity if we approach the biographies of the saints as if — salva reverentia — we were parting the curtains of the Kingdom of Heaven to see each saint perform his miraculous "turns."

The perspective of Heaven is surer, for the number of miracles a saint worked on earth are not totted up for his "place," as an examiner might tot up the marks. Above all the angels and saints, the Blessed Virgin Mary is enthroned in light eternal: and the only miracle in her life was the miracle of *herself*.

Yes, that is the point. The greatest miracle in the life of a saintly man is the miracle of himself: the greatest wonder — the only wonder which really impresses the angels — is the wonder of sanctifying grace in the soul of a saint.

It is with great caution that we approach the relation of the

wealth of wonders in the life of Martin de Porres. We prepare
the way for them by a great emphasis on the miracles that were
his virtues.

What Martin brought to Santo Domingo, then, was a deep and
clear simplicity. One of the first things he learned was that great
truth which is the consolation of all religious — that the rule of
their order or congregation is for them the clear and undoubted
expression of the will of God.

With a simple glance of the soul, Martin saw that truth in all
its fullness. The rule was the will of God for the brethren, and
when he was dealing with them, he had only to do what the rule
said in order to do the will of God.

It was as simple as that. And so the trouble began, for there
were some very good men among the Dominicans of Santo Domingo who liked to amend the rule in some of its minor details.

There was, for instance, a certain Br. James, who thought the
rule's taste in hair-cutting was decidedly naive. Now, the trouble
was this. Dr. de Rivero was also a hair-dresser, and so Martin
had learned the art from him. He knew how to handle comb and
scissors, and the prior, discovering this, put him into the care of
Br. Vincent for a day or so, that he might learn the rule's idea of
how comb and scissors should be used. Martin soon learned and
was soon at work on his own. All went clippingly, till one morning Br. James rushed into have a quick hair-trim before class
began.

Br. James came of a very wealthy family in Lima, and was
studying for the priesthood. It is said that those who relinquish
rank and position for an ideal often keep some little extravagance
as a memento of their dead selves.

For Br. James, it was a certain elegance in the cut of his hair.
Br. James was a very clever young man, a brilliant and methodical
student, and you seldom met him around the cloisters without an
open book and an abstracted air.

He brought both with him to Martin's little hair-cutting room
on the particular morning of which we speak. He settled himself

briskly in the chair, opened his book, and said in his most business-like way: "See you do it quickly, Martin. I've much to do this morning. I take it Br. Vincent has told you how I like mine cut?"

"Yes, Br. James," came the meek answer.

Every member of the Dominican household knew how Br. James liked his hair cut, but they allowed him his little wavering from the beaten track; for, after all, he was a very clever young man and a coming light of his order.

Martin knew what the Rule said, and that for Martin was that. So he began to clip, mercilessly, with the fervor of a vocation. Br. James' tonsorial ideas were being clipped away, and the naivety of the rule was rapidly taking their place.

Meantime, Br. James was deeply engrossed in a page of beautiful scholastic tussle between the Thomists and the Scotists. The sound of the scissors in his brain might as well have been the neat clipping of syllogism after syllogism, so little was he aware of his surroundings.

The Thomists had brought forward an argument that seemed utterly conclusive. Now, could the Scotists . . . ? . . . Br. James looked up from the scholastic arena, and saw his own head reflected in the windowpane.

Martin was snipping off the last tuft that stood between Br. James' hair and the strict letter of the law. He jumped to his feet in indignation, scattering syllogisms in the air. The little fool, why did they put a brat of a Black on such a job, anyhow, they should have known better, in future. . . . Br. James voiced his indignation in no uncertain way.

"But, Br. James, I only did what the rule says," Martin protested,, lowering his eyes at his own temerity.

"Oh-ho, so you're going to teach us the rule now, are you? Let me tell you. . . ."

What followed was disconcerting for Br. James and amusing. At one moment, he was storming at the little Black's presumption: at the next, he was looking down at Martin, kneeling at his feet and saying he was sorry he had offended him. An aristocratic echo in Br. James' mind told him that it does not do to be soft with these Blacks, so he continued to storm.

Then, according to one of Martin's biographers, a delicious thing happened. From the pocket of his white "habit," Martin produced a nice, juicy orange, and held it up to Br. James — presumably that he might suck himself into sweeter tolerance of the rule! It was too much for him, and he left in high dudgeon, muttering something about "in future."

Martin rose from his knees with a sigh. It was a pity Br. James was so vexed. He wondered how he would react the next time, for he would cut it exactly the same way. The rule said so, and a thousand "in future's" from Br. James couldn't alter the will of God as thus expressed for Martin.

In a short time, however, Br. James became reconciled to the new regime, for it was hard to reason with a mind that was such a straight, logical line of utter simplicity.

"The Rule is the will of God, Br. James — even the will of God about hair-cutting." There was no answer to that. It is hard to be logically faced with a choice between a few curls and the will of God.

This, we said, is a chapter which is to concern itself chiefly with the virtues of Martin de Porres, lest they be lost sight of in the crowding up of wonders. We have noticed this great simplicity. Besides it, we place his lovely virtue of courtesy.

We are told that Francis of Assisi ran after a beggar to apologize to him. Martin de Porres went one better. As we shall see later, he apologized to a rat for not having fed it.

To place courtesy among the virtues, and to underline it as one of the chief virtues of a holy man may seem an exaggeration. Yet the appreciation of the bouquet of a wine is already the highest praise of the wine itself: and courtesy is the bouquet, the aroma, of the perfect blend of virtues that we call a Christian gentleman. The saint is, by definition, pre-eminently that.

We speak of the virtue of courtesy. Christ reduced the whole law and the prophets to the love of God and the love of one's neighbor for God. You could define charity-to-the-neighbor in terms similar to Newman's famous definition of a gentleman, as a wariness never to give unnecessary pain. Such wariness shows itself in courtesy: for courtesy is the face which charity shows to the world. You can read the grace of God in that face. You can read courtesy in all the actions of Martin de Porres.

But we must examine this idea of the virtue of courtesy a little further, lest we seem to praise the false veneer which goes under its name. Courtesy is no veneer. Nor is it a nicely-toned benevolence of mood which you breathe around you as a proper atmosphere for your dress suit or your mink coat.

It is quite likely that the Pharisees presented a fine surface of politeness to the world: but in the eyes of Christ, that surface became a whited slab, hiding rottenness and dead men's bones. As a badge of class, the soul of courtesy leaves its body of politeness, and you have the rottenness which is the vice of snobbery.

You meet the virtue of courtesy in its charming littleness, when you join the group on the lakeside after the Resurrection, and meet the lovely courtesy of the opportunity given to St. Peter to cancel a triple denial by a triple confession. For Christ, the God-Man, was by very definition the most courteous of men. Belloc has written splendidly:

> "Of courtesy, it is much less
> Than courage of heart or holiness;
> Yet, in my walks it seems to me
> That the grace of God is in courtesy."

Well may we look for it, then, in the faces of our saints.

This virtue of courtesy will be evident in every action of St. Martin. But we shall anticipate in time here and bring forward a small incident that will serve to raise the corner of the veil on his lovely courtesy. Just such a raising of the veil is the trivial incident of the mantilla.

It is a lovely little incident, first because it brings Martin and his sister Jane together for a moment in the story. We left Jane with her uncle in Guayaquil, and now when we visit her again, she is in Lima, happily married and with a little daughter called Catherine.

Now, Catherine wanted a mantilla. Every fashionable young lady in Lima wore a mantilla, and she felt out of the picture. She was nearly fourteen now and felt quite grown-up. When her Uncle Martin asked her what present she would like, the young girl asked for a mantilla because she wanted to look her best among the other girls. She was not rebuked for vanity by her wonder-working uncle, but Martin promised simply to do his best.

Martin's was a very busy life, in which such a promise would surely be forgotten. But not so — for it is essential to true courtesy that promises like that should not be forgotten. Catherine got her mantilla — in fact, she got the pick of six.

Having, then, looked at the virtues that lay behind the wonders, we now pass on to a chapter of wonders, always remembering, however, that the virtues are and must remain for us the real wonders.

5.   A CHAPTER OF WONDERS

Lima woke each morning with a riot of bells. The cathedral sent its deep-throated ball of sound hopping from roof to roof of the sleeping houses; sharp needles of sound made holes in the mist around the Franciscan friary; St. Peter Nolasco's bronze bell spoke deep and sensibly, as though it chided as an age-old grandsire would; San Sebastian fussed and jangled its call to prayer.

But before any of these bells had cleared its throat, the bell of the monastery tower in Santo Domingo had pealed forth at five o'clock to waken the brethren to a new day. Martin de Porres rose from his hard bed and reached for his shoes, for — like the brethren — that was the only part of his clothing he took off at night.

We are told that his morning ritual was something like this. Facing his crucifix, he bowed down and said: "Praised be Jesus Christ!" Then he turned to where he knew a picture of our Lady and a picture of St. Dominic hung on his wall.

We are told that his morning prayer was: "Dear Blessed Mother, let me be useful this day. Holy Father St. Dominic, help me in my work. St. Joseph, pray for all of us in this monastery, and keep us from harm."

A beautiful prayer which made those first moments of the day as incense rising before the throne of God. It was the spiritual counterpart of the roses in the monastery garden that were breathing their perfume on the first breezes of the morning darkness.

The last echoes of the morning bell were still playing hide-and-seek among the stone arches as Martin hurried along a corridor full of the chilly fingers of the morning. For Martin was one of those of whom the Psalmist says: "As the eyes of the handmaid are on the hands of her master, so are my eyes on You, O Lord my God." He knew that his Master's command was in the sound of that bell, and he would obey that command almost before it was spoken.

He went towards one of the several chapels in which he was privileged to serve Mass. When we think of his utter simplicity and of his deep appreciation of spiritual realities, it must surely have been an inspiring sight to see Martin de Porres serving Mass. To do so is a great privilege for the layman, but it is one of which familiarity can very easily breed an absence of wonder. But the wonder of it all was always fresh for Martin de Porres.

That is the secret of the freshness of his soul — and indeed of the souls of all the saints. They never lost their sense of wonder, above all, their sense of wonder at the Incarnation, the Redemption, and the daily morning miracle of the Mass in our midst.

Thus sanctified at their source, the hours of his day began to flow. There were dishes to be washed, cloisters to be swept, linen to be folded, the garden to be tended, and a thousand other little daily jobs, not one of them too small for the full devotion of Martin.

If Martin de Porres' sanctity sometimes showed itself in wonders, they were the exception, for he was like many other masters of holiness in doing ordinary things extraordinarily well and finding in them the stuff of his halo.

There was one particular morning when Martin finished his house duties and hurried out to the garden. It was one of those mornings when, as the poet said, Spring would move her incense-laden thurible even among the tombs.

There was the praise of God in the song of the birds, in the perfume of the flowers, in the glistening dew-pearls that hung on the blades of grass — and, for Martin de Porres, in the glistening eyes of a rat looking from the mouth of its den. His soul sang, as he moved through it all, and in that singing it was lifted as a thing of beauty to the throne of God. Yes, even the glistening eyes of the rat were so lifted.

But there was one man that morning who did not place the rats on his list of motives for joining in the cosmic hymn of the Psalmist. This was the sacristan, Br. Michael. He had hurried from his breakfast with plans made for a very busy day.

He would inspect and shake out all the linen. All went well till he pulled out a surplice — and found it full of holes. An alb followed, equally riddled. Then an altar-cloth, like a sieve — and so on, with a dozen of Br. Michael's more precious possessions.

Disgusted, he dropped them in a heap on the table and went in search of the prior. The prior listened, clicked his tongue in annoyance. "Rats!" said Br. Michael with venom. "Rats!" agreed the prior, with equal venom. Then Br. Michael said "Rats" again for good measure and they stood looking at each other.

"Go and tell Martin he must do something about them," the prior said.

Had you asked the prior at that moment what he thought Martin could do about them, he would have said that really he didn't know, but that somehow when you had lived with Martin for a while you naturally said that sort of thing when there seemed no solution.

Br. Michael hurried away in search of him, still muttering about rats and linen. As he hurried into the garden, he noticed neither flowers nor birds nor sunshine. His whole mental and emotional horizon at that moment contained nothing else save rats and linen.

Meantime, Martin had moved on to his own special plot. The prior had allowed him some ground in which to grow herbs which he could use in making medicine and ointments for the community and for the poor who thronged the doors of Santo Domingo.

"Ah, Br. Michael," he beamed, "praise be God for such a lovely day. I was just getting ready to plant some special poppy seed for a cure I — —"

"Oh, poppy me no poppies," retorted Michael. "You'll talk about nice weather and poppies while the rats are eating the linen for the holy services!"

For, by dint of brooding on rats and linen, Br. Michael had almost come to the point of blaming Martin for it all, and his tone need not have been varied had Martin been standing there convicted of having himself nibbled the linen in his spare time.

"Rats, Br. Michael?" Martin answered.

"Yes, I said rats. Put down that stupid digger and come and see the abomination of desolation they have made."

Martin went and saw. He looked at one piece after another, with a rueful expression on his face. Br. Michael said "Rats" several times.

Then Martin said something which drove everything else out of his mind.

"It's all my fault," he said dolefully, "for not having fed the rats."

Br. Michael's eyes opened wide in amazement. He threw up his hands, said he gave up, and went off to tell the prior that, as far as he could make out, Martin de Porres was in league with the rats.

Meantime, Martin returned to his herbs. As he bent down, feeling the kindly soil about his feet and the warmth of the sun on his back, he felt brotherly towards all nature, and try as he would he was unable to stir up in himself a due and proper indignation against the rats.

He had fed stray dogs and stray cats and had poulticed and bandaged a hare: but never had he given as much as a crumb to the poor rats. The poor things had been neglected and they had to eat something. But what could he do to cure their appetite for

Br. Michael's linen? By now, Martin had convinced himself that it really was all his fault.

But what, indeed? Most of us would have thought of traps and terriers and guns and knobby sticks. Not so, Martin. They were God's creatures and his courtesy extended even to them. But how was he to cure them? He worried over it as he planted his seeds.

Then suddenly, he straightened and said — "Yes, I'll do that." He was smiling with great relief. The problem was solved. He laid down his seeds, dry-washed the clay from his hands, and went off to have a chat with one of the rats. The solution was just as simple as that!

Now, where had he seen a rat last? Yes, in the garden an hour or so since, there was one which had formed part of his morning lifting up of nature to God. He had an idea where that gentleman lived, so he paid him a call. When the rat heard Martin's voice, it came to him immediately.

"Good morning," Martin said. "I came to see you about that linen of Br. Michael's that you and your friends have been eating. Now, I'm not blaming you, for it's all my fault for not having fed you. But I want to make a bargain with you. If you agree to get all the rats to leave the monastery and live in the old disused barn, I promise to feed you every day."

Well, that was fair enough. We do not know whether the rat nodded or squeaked his assent, but we do know that he understood his role as pied-piper of Santo Domingo. Martin returned to the monastery.

On the doorstep, he met Br. Michael. Well, Br. Michael asked, had he got any solution for the rat problem yet. Yes, Martin answered, he had just had a talk with a rat and he thought there wouldn't be any more trouble. You see, it was all his fault for not feeding them, and now they would live in a sort of community in the old barn and he would feed them.

Martin moved on. Br. Michael looked after him in amazement. It would be an anachronism to say that Br. Michael said "Nuts" in his own mind: but it is a safe guess that he said something equivalent in seventeenth century Spanish.

But, to the amazement of the whole community, all the rats — "fathers, mothers, uncles, cousins" — did leave the monastery and took up residence in the old barn, as gentlefolk of leisure to be fed daily by Martin. A bead had been added to Martin's string of wonders.

Some of the brethren were not surprised at this, when they looked back to certain things Martin had done. Like St. Francis of Assisi, he seemed to have a sympathetic hand on the pulse of all nature. It had already been apparent in simpler things, of which the pied-pipering of the rats had been but the culmination.

There had been that day, for instance, when Martin had put a stray dog, and a stray cat eating from the same dish. That was wonderful enough. But he saw a mouse, assured it that it also was one of God's creatures, and enticed it to the dish. The three ate from the same dish in perfect harmony. It was quite a common sight to see Martin returning from the town with two or three strays about his feet.

The prior had another great worry, and once again, he turned to Martin. It was to be expected that Martin, with Dr. de Rivero's dispensary as his background, should very soon have been put in charge of the sick.

But there was one very sick priest to whom Martin had not yet been sent. This was Father Peter Monteadosca, who lay upstairs in agony with a poisoned leg. The prior had just received the news that the good father must lose his leg. He was walking along the cloister where Martin was sweeping, and he stopped to tell him the news.

"He is upstairs, Martin, in such great pain that he cannot bear anyone in the room with him. I want you to go to him and do as best you can."

Once again, it was an instinctive turning to the little Black servant when everything else seemed useless.

Once again, Martin was handed a problem. As he finished his

sweeping, he wondered what he could do. If he could take him something that would please him and put him in better humor, then maybe Father Peter would allow him to remain in the room. Martin knew very well about the whims and fancies of the sick. If he could only discover what whim had taken Father Peter at this moment.

Only God knew that — so he would ask God. Martin prayed. Then he decided on the first nice thing that happened to occur to him, and characteristically enough, it was from the garden. He would take a nice fresh salad to him, and hope for the best.

Now, it happened that if there was one thing Father Peter wished for at that moment, besides the curing of his leg, it was a nice salad. When Martin knocked on his door and entered, he grumbled as usual that he wanted nobody but only to be left in peace with his agony. Martin said soothingly:

"I don't want to disturb you, Father, but I thought you might like a salad."

At the word "salad" the old man levered himself painfully up in the bed, with a look of surprise and joy on his face.

"Eh, how did you know I wanted a salad? I've been telling myself for the past hour that they won't bring me anything I can eat — a nice salad, for instance. And now, you come with one."

The good father set to work on the salad with a great good will. Meantime, Martin ventured gingerly to unwind the bandage on the leg, looked up now and then as though expecting a bellow. But Father Peter was very docile at the moment, so he let Martin wash and rebandage the leg.

A few hours later, Father Peter was walking about his room, stamping gleefully on the leg which, a few hours before, he could not put under him. He sang the praises of Martin to all the brethren, saying that he had been miraculously cured.

Martin himself just smiled, saying that there was nothing miraculous in water and a bandage, but that God must love Father Peter very much seeing that He cured him so quickly.

We have brought forward two wonders in this chapter for the

special reason that they spring immediately from that great simplicity which we have noted as the foundation virtue of Blessed Martin's soul.

There are greater wonders yet to be told of him: there is even the raising of the dead. But we must pause for a moment to savor the two we have listed.

They are wonders wrought by childlike simplicity: by that simple faith in the fatherhood and goodness of God which Christ said would move mountains. Yet, few of us would consider our faith strong and simple enough to do either of these wonders. They are, of course, for the chosen souls. In every age, God raises up such chosen souls to prove that the great truths He preached can be realized in all their literal simplicity in human lives.

Martin de Porres was raised up to underline the great truth that Heaven can be commanded by a childlike soul.

6. "FRIEND, GO UP HIGHER"

The monastery of Santo Domingo was sinking in debt and its prior was a very worried man indeed. Ceaseless prayer went up to Heaven from the community that God might send the necessary aid. Yet every day brought little else save fresh debts.

Martin de Porres worried over it, but no solution would come. He could, perhaps, go out and work. But where in Lima would he get anyone to employ him; for everyone looked down on the Blacks and considered them fit only to be slaves. The Lima St. Martin knew was a society in which social distinctions were cast-iron, for Lima was very conscious of a ragged beginning which it was determined to live down.

Hence, its mood was resolutely White and resolutely "civilized." The Whites were still few in number, and hence they were very reluctant to have dealings with any of the colored people, who they knew were smouldering not far below the surface, about their loss of ancient freedoms. The stage, therefore, was completely set against the chance of decent employment for Martin, and he knew it. There was nothing for it but to worry and pray.

Of late, the prior had left the monastery more and more frequently with a parcel under his arm. Martin knew what this meant — something from the monastery had to be sacrificed that a bill might be paid.

117

The prior had two beautiful pictures of which he was very fond. They hung in the refectory, framed in magnificent Spanish oak, beautifully gilt. The prior had taken Martin to see them on many occasions, for he loved to talk about their beauty and Martin made an excellent listener. Martin soon knew and loved every detail of those pictures.

He remembered especially one evening when a rose sunset had seeped through the windows and the pictures hung in its glory. The prior had called him. "Come, Martin, and see the pictures. They are like scenes taking place in the heart of a sunset." Martin never forgot the beauty of those pictures as he saw them then, nor the radiant joy of the prior's face as he looked at them.

Martin had seen that face very often of late when there was no radiance in it, but a November greyness of anxiety. That was when he watched him leaving the monastery with the parcel under his arm.

Then one morning, Martin saw something which chilled all the joy of the day for him as though a damp hand had been laid on his heart. He was sweeping a corridor, when, glancing out, he saw the prior leaving the garden with two big parcels. Martin got one glimpse of his face — tired, worn, defeated — and his heart went out to him.

Dropping his brush, he ran to the refectory. The two pictures were gone. The marks on the wall looked like torn skin. It was a suggestive thought. For to part with that treasure was as grievous to the prior as if someone had torn his skin.

Plunged in sorrow, Martin stood looking at the place where the treasure had been. Then, like a ray of light suddenly cutting the darkness, an idea came to him. As usual, it was a drastically simple one, and provided such an immediate solution to the problem that Martin laughed for very joy of it.

He was strong, capable, educated, all-round — and therefore, he would fetch quite a high price as a slave. Like a man from whom the whole weary burden of life has suddenly slipped, he skipped down the stairs and went after the prior.

By this time, the prior was struggling up a hill towards the market. His burden was getting heavier with every step, and his heart was heavier still. It is hard to sacrifice a thing of beauty with which you have so long lived and about which you have woven so many dreams that it has become, as it were, part of the texture of your own soul.

And that is what the prior was doing at this moment. He was thinking how fitting it was that there should be a hill to climb, and he was uniting his sacrifice with that of Calvary, when he heard a patter of feet behind him. He turned and saw Martin — hot, breathless, radiant.

"There's no need to sell them, Father. Sell me, Martin, and you'll find you'll get the price of many, many pictures for me, and you'll be able to pay the monastery debts. It's so simple a solution, Father Prior."

The prior stood amazed. . . . How true it is that we never or very seldom really know those with whom we are in daily, shoulder-brushing contact. For a character, after all, is like a landscape. You think you see and know it whole and entire at a single glance. But the morning fog lifts, and you see new vistas, with wider and unsuspected horizons.

So, too, you may think you know a man, and then some day he may do something which really reveals his character to you and you may stand amazed. . . .

The prior of Santo Domingo stood amazed, as he looked for the first time into the depths of a soul. It is in moments of revelation like these that one sees the truth of those words of a very great poet: "A terrible beauty is born." And suddenly a weight lifted from the prior's heart, and the heavy parcels seemed already lighter on his arms.

He leaned his pictures against a wall, and put his hand on Martin's shoulder.

"No, Martin," he said, "you must not think of that. You are more precious than all earthly beauty."

Martin was troubled and made as though he would plead. This

must surely have been the most amazing moment in the prior's life.

In the dust and the heat of a Liman morning, a man stood before him pleading to be sold into slavery. "Greater love than this no man has . . ." The words came floating to him through the heat and the dust.

A jewel of a human soul had been entrusted to him, and he would foster and cherish it. How light seemed all worries, when you had a life in your midst that mirrored the generosity of Christ. All this, the prior thought as he stood looking at Martin: but he said only —

"Come now, Martin. No more of this about selling yourself. Come, help me with these to the market."

The prior felt happier and comforted, as a man should who, setting off heartsore and despondent, meets with God-like charity on the way. . . . And he praised God for Martin de Porres.

Back in the monastery, the prior called Martin to him.

"Martin, I have prayed to God about you for quite a time, and now it has pleased Him to give me a wonderful answer to my prayer. I am going to make you a lay brother of the First Order of St. Dominic."

Had the prior called him and slapped his face, Martin could not have been more stunned. He stammered. He protested.

But this time, the prior was deaf to all protests. His decision had been taken when he stood dazzled with beauty in the prosaic drabness of a Liman street. This decision was for Martin the clear will of God. He received it with thankful joy and a deep humility.

Martin's work was to continue the same. There would be the same daily routine of sweeping and weeding, of tending the sick, of feeding the poor at the doors, of attending to the stray dog that limped and to the bird that fluttered to his feet with its wing broken. But now, the hand that performed all these tasks was a consecrated hand: consecrated by the vows of Poverty, of Chastity, and of Obedience.

7. THE SERVANT OF ALL

"Charity is patient, is kind. . . ." It would need to be when dealing with that pushing throng of poor who crowded to the door of Santo Domingo.

Father Malachy, that delightful creation of Bruce Marshall, found it helped a lot to close his eyes when meditating in a crowded compartment on the love of our neighbor.

Practical charity to the neighbor means getting your two arms to the elbows in the suds of human nature, as a woman does in the suds of her washing. And you cannot do that without splashing yourself unpleasantly and feeling the grime on your hands.

Anything else is a kind of kidgloved spiritual dilettantism, which, while it will not go without its reward, is not the robust thing we call the charity of the saints.

Martin de Porres was growing old in charity to the poor. Every day, he hurried through his meal that he might the sooner come to the poor: for Martin had grasped the truth that service to the poor is service to Christ, in all its deep simplicity, and he would keep Christ waiting on his doorstep as short a time as at all possible.

His appearance at the door was greeted with great joy. It was not just that he brought with him a basket of food — though, of course, there was that. There was something else. He brought his

121

own glowing heart that knew how to speak a word of comfort to many whose path was strewn mainly with the thorns of life. The smile with which Martin greeted the poor had nothing of condescension in it, but was warm with the full, rich warmness of the charity of Christ.

"May the Lord bless and increase this food, and satisfy all those who come." This was Martin's simple blessing over the food. For at least an hour, Martin stood at the door giving out food, and every hand stretched out to him was the Hand of Christ to his eyes of faith.

That was the stupendously simple explanation of why Martin never glanced into his basket to calculate his charity, and the food just continued to be there as long as he wanted it. To the eye of an onlooker, the food in that basket never seemed to get less. They had come to him like hungry sheep crowding to their pastor, and once again the power of holiness to echo an action of Christ was shown to the world.

Christ in the desert: Martin on the doorstep of his monastery, through the power of Christ. The smile of Christ with the blessing of those loaves: the mirroring of that smile on the lips of Martin de Porres. For he whose soul was redolent of his Master's charity could command that all-powerful Hand again over the loaves in Lima, as It had shadowed the loaves in the desert when the Christian world was being born.

Martin had made a pact with the rats. When the last of the poor had been fed, he closed the door, and "gathering up the fragments that remained" he made his way towards the old barn. The rats had to be fed for a promise was a promise even when made to a rat.

The novices, whom Martin saw coming into the monastery as schoolboys and growing to the crowning dignity of the priesthood, knew the warmth of his charity. Sometimes there would be a little feast of cake and fruit waiting for them in Martin's room when class had finished, though often on these occasions they had to keep quiet so as not to disturb the sick Black or Indian who had been brought home by Martin to rest on his own bed.

In particular, we are told, there was a tall, stately, brilliant young priest called Father Cyprian de Medina, whom Martin sometimes watched as he moved about the cloisters reading his books.

In his quiet doing of God's will, the years had stolen by unnoticed for Martin, though they flecked his raven hair with white and stooped his shoulders. Martin remembered that tall, stately priest when he was neither tall nor stately, but fat and small and shy and clumsy and depressed.

The youngster would come to Martin when others had laughed at his clumsiness, to pour his sorrow out to him. The load of depression would suddenly seem light in the warmth of charity with which Martin would greet him. It would take the form of comforting words, sometimes backed up by a juicy orange.

Now, Martin would look at that stately figure and praise God for a good priest: and Father Cyprian would look at the little black figure stooped over a bush, and praise God for the man who helped him to His holy altar.

There was also a certain Father John who, as a novice, had been sick in bed with a high fever. His door had been locked for the night, and the long hours of darkness dragged themselves painfully across his wakefulness. He was parched for a drink, and in pain he spoke aloud, calling for Martin — the name that was nearest to every novice's lips when there was need of comforting.

When he opened his eyes a moment later, Martin stood by his bed with a drink and with some fresh sheets. Martin, Father John insisted, must have passed through the door to come to him.

Perhaps, someone suggested to Father John, he had done so without leaving his room. There had been some strange whisperings about Martin's power of bilocation. A stranger had once startled them by declaring publicly that Martin had befriended him when he was a sick prisoner in Moorish Algiers. A sea-captain declared he had met Martin in China and Martin had others who claimed to be his debtors in Mexico, in Japan, in the Philippines.

Certain it is that Martin had tears for all in sorrow, and his soul had so grown in Christ-like sensitivity, that it may very well have transcended the laws of time and space to answer a call on its charity. For these things are possible with God.

Whispers of new and surprising wonders were abroad concerning the little black lay brother. When the Rimac river was in dangerous flood, a prayer of Martin's had caused it to sink quickly to its accustomed banks.

One of the fathers, entering the monastery chapel at a quiet hour, had seen Br. Martin raised from the ground in ecstatic prayer before the crucifix.

On a lesser scale, but as wonderful in its way, was the news the novices could tell after a country walk with Br. Martin. At one moment they were miles from the monastery, and within a few minutes of the time for prayer. At the next, they were beside the monastery.

Behind all these wonders was a prayer, so Godlike in its simplicity that it could move mountains. And the man who offered that prayer continued to feed the poor, to sweep the cloisters, to keep his promise to a rat. . . .

It is interesting at some stage in a man's life to look at him surrounded by his friends. When Martin de Porres died, the whole of Lima claimed him as its friend. But every man, in his walk through life, makes some special friends, necessarily few since real friendship is as rare as it is priceless.

It would seem impossible that the same town at the same time should have been sanctified by a twin-soul to Martin de Porres. Yet this was true. The Dominicans had another monastery in Lima in which another lay brother — John Masias — lived.

Six years younger than Martin, he had come to South America while in his teens, and soon afterward had consecrated his life to God in the Dominican Order. We know him today as Blessed John Masias, for the same simplicity and charity has placed a halo about his name which links him eternally with St. Martin de

Porres. Martin formed a deep spiritual friendship with John.

It is refreshing, in a jaded world, to picture these two friends together, when Martin had come to visit John and they sat together under the trees. They would discuss ways and means of extending yet further the fruits of that love for the neighbor which inspired them.

Martin was troubled about the number of young girls who, on account of the condition of things in Lima, were exposed to a life of sin. Br. John suggested that perhaps Martin's friend Don Mateo would provide the money to aid these girls with a dowry so that they could get married; and to educate some of them to become nuns.

Don Mateo was a man of influence in society and he was Martin's friend. Martin had many friends in Lima society, for many had known the blessing he brought with him.

Martin had another friend in Lima — the lovely Rose de Flores. St. Rose's life is strangely parallel in its aims and ideals with that of Martin. When Martin brought his basket of food to the poor, he was very careful to deal tactfully with a little group who stood apart — the servants of down-at-heel gentry.

Listen to this, from one of St. Rose's most graceful biographers, Margaret T. Munro in her book — *Unlikely Saints*: "Two classes of people made an especial appeal to Rose, women who had come down in the world, and abandoned Indian women — abandoned often in every sense of the word. Rose did much to seek out and help women who had been well off but were now all but starving behind a brave façade of appearances. Such help has to be given with the utmost secrecy and is always one of the stiffest problems in the path of charity."

How dear must all that have made her to Martin de Porres. They called her "La Rosita," and her charity indeed had the fragrance of a rose.

They were stirring times in Lima. "When Rose was about twenty-five or twenty-six," writes Margaret Munro, "there took place, not exactly a native rising, but a sudden withdrawal of the natives from the religion of their conquerors. But the idolatry to which they returned was an idolatry shorn of all its sweeter aspects; everywhere the revolt was an uprush of the dark powers of the human heart. A further note of terror was added when a village of lapsed people were swallowed by an earthquake. But terror is catching. The dark wave swept through the country, sucking down natives and Whites alike. The clergy were helpless against its satanic power. At this juncture there came to Lima another saint, St. Francis Solano" (*op. cit.*, p. 107).

It is easy to see from this glimpse at the world St. Martin and St. Rose knew, that the exercise of charity in Lima of the seventeenth century called for great heroism. With Rose, charity also took the form of scourgings to blood in expiation for the sins of men. Her wonderful example must have been a strength and an inspiration to Martin de Porres.

Perhaps it was because those two rooms her parents allowed her in which to house people suffering from revolting diseases were full, or perhaps it was pressure from her parents, that made Rose set off one day in quest of Martin. She had met with steady opposition from her parents and family who considered that her charity should stop this side of bringing disease into the house.

Whenever Rose felt discouraged or depressed, she would seek out Martin and he would comfort her. He understood her, and saw deep down into the ideals and motives which inspired all she did. Whenever, then, she had a patient to whom she could not herself attend, she was sure of being helped by her friend, Martin de Porres.

Meantime, the wonders of Martin continued to multiply, and the crown of them all has yet to be related. One day, Martin returned to Santo Domingo and found that a pall of sorrow had descended on the community in his absence. Death always spreads a certain hush around it. There were the subdued voices, the muffled footsteps, the sense of sudden emptiness, the serious and prayerful faces. All these seemed to greet Martin at once, with the news that Br. Thomas was dead.

They told him he had called for Martin many times in the delirium of his agony. Then, he is really dead — you are sure of it? Martin wanted to know. Why, of course, they answered, and they seemed to think Martin was being unnecessarily stupid and silly to doubt it. . . . "And they laughed him to scorn." Interesting, how these echoes of Gospel detail seem to multiply themselves in the lives of the saints.

They were surprised that Martin took it all so calmly. When he asked to be taken immediately to Br. Thomas, a deeper hush — the hush of strange expectancy — settled on the brethren. Br. Ferdinand accompanied him to the room.

Outside, none of the priests or brothers voiced his hope, but each one nourished it in the secret places of his heart. Father John's thoughts may very well have been back at that night when Martin came through a locked door to answer his fever-parched calls.

Br. Thomas had died with Martin's name as the last human words on his lips. The rest had been his prayer, repeated after the voice that spoke it urgently in his ear. Yet, Br. Thomas had died giving the impression that his soul was still calling for Martin. Would even the grave keep Martin from a soul that was calling him?

In the room, things happened quickly and with an awful simplicity. Martin had knelt before the crucifix in prayer. Then, before the amazed eyes of Br. Ferdinand, he had risen, taken the clay-cold hand of the corpse, and said: "In the Name of Jesus Christ, Br. Thomas, arise." Immediately, the warmth and softness of living flesh told of the soul's presence, and Br. Thomas sat up.

"Ah, Br. Thomas," Martin greeted him, "you must be hungry after your long sleep." He went immediately to a little locker in the room and brought out some food. Br. Thomas was sitting up in bed, eating some food, even before his eyes had had time to notice the signs of mourning around him. Martin quietly opened the shutters and left the room.

Martin hurried. He had something to do — had forgotten something — it may even have been to feed the rats. To the death-hushed community waiting in the corridor, he said simply:

"Br. Thomas is well again. He is sitting up having something to eat."

The grave had not been a match for the urgent charity of Martin de Porres.

8. AND THE REST IS . . .

The wonder of a resurrection in their midst had set the brethren talking of the wonder God had so quietly and so simply placed among them. There is a swiftness and angelic speed about charity, so that St. Paul could not speak to the Corinthians about it without a breathless tumbling of phrase on phrase. When the saints advance in age, they are subject to all the infirmity that flesh is heir to: but the life of their soul is a steady flame of charity, ever growing in intensity, always young.

Strange things continued to be told of Br. Martin. A young Spaniard called John Vasquez had come to live with the Dominicans. Martin had found him, friendless and penniless, in Lima, and had taken him home to share his own room. The youth had become very attached to Martin, who surrounded him with all the warmth of a parent's love.

One morning, after a night in which the tremors of an earthquake had given the community an anxious time, John Vasquez came into the sacristy to tell the brother there of a wonder that had swallowed up his fear of the earthquake in a greater fear.

He had been asleep in the little bed which Martin had made up for him in his room, when he was awakened, as much by a strange light in the room as by the trembling of the floor. Opening his eyes, he was utterly perplexed, for the room was in daylight, and when he saw the darkness of midnight heaping itself against the window above his head, he was really frightened.

He turned quickly in the bed to call for Martin, and saw him lying on the floor with the brightness of day about him. John, now thoroughly shaken, jumped from the bed and began to pull Martin's arm, sobbing and calling his name. He could not attract his attention. The coldness of the floor was under his feet, and a cold hand of fear at his heart.

He went back quickly to bed, pulled the clothes over his head and sobbed himself to sleep. In the morning, Martin had called him — and he was the same Martin, with the same black face and the same smile. It was all so strange.

The brother had continued to fold the vestments as he listened to the tale, and a little smile played about his lips. When the lad had finished, he turned to him and said:

"Let me assure you that nothing that Br. Martin does need frighten nor even surprise you. Listen here, John. I have seen him pass swiftly through the cloisters like a *living ball of fire.*"

Christ has said: "I have come to cast fire on the earth, and what do I desire but that it be enkindled." A soul like that of Martin de Porres was as tinder to that fire of Divine Love cast on earth, and when it pleased God to manifest the glowing heart of His servant, it was fitting that the symbol should have been a swift ball of flame.

There were others who told how they had seen four angels with Martin as he went about his duties. In the cool of the evening of his day, the angels walked with Martin, for his conversation was always with them. Perhaps it was from them that he gained that knowledge of the Bible and even of the Angelic Doctor's teaching which so amazed those who sometimes brought their doubts to him.

Meantime, Martin swept his cloisters, consoled the sick, fed the poor, continued to keep his promise to the rat; for the halos of the saints can be woven of the meanest and lowliest of life's duties, no less than by the most spectacular preaching and teaching with voice and pen.

As he plied his sweeping-brush, however, there came more and more frequently to Martin, certain stabs of pain which caused him to grip the handle, lean heavily on it, and stand still in pain.

Martin knew that they were the warning fingers of death — he would have called it life, new life — reaching out feelingly towards him. Had Martin de Porres been able to grasp those fingers, it would have been in a clasp of welcome.

One day, however, a priest who loved Martin as he did his own soul, saw him in the grip of pain. Full of alarm, he came to him and insisted that he should go immediately to his room and lie down for a while.

Martin left his brush aside and took the advice given him. By so simple an incident was it shown that the end was near, for with characters like Martin de Porres a concession to pain could mean only one thing.

Shortly after this, Father Cyprian — the priest who owed so much to Martin's kindness — came to him with some startling news. His Grace the Archbishop of Mexico, Don Felician de Vega, had fallen sick while on a visit to Lima, and had attributed his speedy cure to the prayers of Br. Martin.

Now, when beginning his preparations for the return journey, he had decided to ask that Br. Martin should be allowed to accompany him, that he might have him always at hand for prayer and advice.

Father Cyprian, as the archbishop's nephew, had received the first news of this, and he had hastened to tell Martin. The old brother received the news with a smile. It was a quiet smile that made Father Cyprian feel somehow uncomfortable. He wondered what it could mean. He had not long to wait for an answer.

One morning, Martin appeared dressed in a brand new habit. The community was amazed, for Br. Martin had all his life insisted on wearing the most patched, worn-out habits he could find.

They used to joke lightheartedly with him about his belonging to the "green" section of the order, on account of the age of the habits he wore. Now one of them challenged him jokingly:

"How now, Martin, are you getting vain in your old age?"

"I'm sure it's not worth getting vain now," Martin laughed. And, seriously, he added: "I just thought I would like a new one for my burial."

Martin's companion stood looking at him in speechless amazement.

"You see, Brother," Martin explained quietly, "I am going to die in about four days."

The good brother rubbed his eyes to see whether he was dreaming. No — it was broad daylight, he was wide awake, and there before him was Martin de Porres calmly announcing the day of his death.

It did not take long for such startling news to reach to every member of the community. There was a tenseness of expectation in those few days. Time had on many occasions shown that Martin's predictions had been true.

This was the first time he had foretold anything about himself and all Lima was soon filled with a bedside expectation of death. Their friend — the friend of poor and of rich — had quietly announced the day of his departure. Father Cyprian remembered that strange little smile and now he knew what it had meant.

Br. Martin took to his bed a day or two later. The news spread through Lima like a panic. Santo Domingo was surrounded by a huge, sorrowing throng of Indians, of Blacks, of Whites, of all those who had felt the charity of Martin de Porres warming the coldness of their lives.

Messages came from the archbishop of Mexico imploring the Dominicans to spare no expense to save him. The king's viceroy, Don Luis Fernandez Bobadilla, arrived post-haste in his splendid carriage, to beg a last word with the servant of God.

While the prior was receiving the viceroy with what ceremony he could, under the extraordinary circumstances, a strange thing happened. Martin, who never made a request, made one now. He asked that he should be left alone and that no visitors should be allowed to come.

The young novice who had been placed near the door to make sure that Br. Martin's wishes were respected, found himself in a very embarrassing position. He saw the prior showing the viceroy, with all pomp and ceremony, towards Martin's door. But he braved the situation.

Stepping forward, he stopped the prior, and shyly made Br. Martin's wishes known. The prior blushed, and was about to insist, when the viceroy said quietly:

"I shall sit down and await his pleasure. It is little in return for the privilege of seeing such an heroic soul once again."

The prior, annoyed at the discourtesy he had been forced into, looked sternly at the novice. The youngster broke down, and began to sob. He said that Br. Martin had invisible visitors, that he was speaking with the Blessed Virgin and St. Dominic. . . . A few minutes later, Martin sent word that he would see anyone whom the prior wished him to receive.

Br. Martin's eyes turned towards the viceroy as he entered the tiny room, and there was welcome and surprise in them. But the viceroy saw neither the welcome nor the surprise: he saw only that the eyes were filled with serene joy, as though they already mirrored the beatitude of the eternal hills.

Before the wonder of those eyes, the rich robes wrinkled on the hard floor as the viceroy sank to his knees and bowed his head on the little black hand that was stretched out feebly to him. His tears were still wet on Br. Martin's hand when he rose, commended himself humbly to his prayers, and left the room with the memory of those eyes deep in his soul.

Half an hour later, Martin de Porres died — if indeed that could be called death which was a smile of welcome to life at its fullest. The chill of death was rather with those who, in a moment, found the world more chilly because the fire of a living charity had been taken from among them.

Lima usually awoke slowly in the coldness of its dawn. But when the solemn death-bell of Santo Domingo spoke its sorrow into the half-light, Lima was quickly wide awake to the tragedy it had awaited. There was scarcely a house to which the sound of the bell came that did not feel that a warmth had been taken from life.

Soon the streets were filled with people, making their way silently towards Santo Domingo. Silently they gathered round the doors of Santo Domingo — men, women, and children, rich and poor, Black and White, all distinction leveled, all snobbery forgotten, conscious only of a blind groping for a precious warmth they had lost. The great bell continued to peal into the morning.

Behind the closed door of the church where the body of Br. Martin lay, a tall and stately priest walked disconsolately up and down the aisle. Every time he came to the remains, he stopped to look earnestly and lovingly at the face that had so often smiled his worries away, at the hand that had rested like a blessing on his arm at moments when life was thorny, at the now silent tongue that was never without the world of cheering encouragement.

It seemed hard that all this should now be frozen in death — that even the flame that was the life of Martin de Porres should now be replaced by that coldness which was like the touch of marble when he laid his hands lovingly on the little black hands he had loved. At last, he could stand it no longer.

"Br. Martin, friend of my soul," he said, gripping the cold hand in his, "your charity was greater than your life, and death cannot have dealt so quickly with it. Let its Christ-like ardor suffuse this frozen flesh, that it may become soft and warm again and we may have the consolation of a sign that you are more than ever with us."

Unconsciously, he had spoken aloud, and scarcely had the words echoed in the empty church than the flesh softened in his grasp and a life-like warmth thawed the whole body.

Father Cyprian sank to his knees, with a Magnificat of joy in his soul. Then the doors were opened, and the news of the wonder changed sorrow into joy, for Martin's body awaited them, warm as his charity.

All day and all night an endless line of people came to kneel at Martin's feet. The body remained warm, and the sight of it brought a great joy and peace to all the beholders.

People put their hands on the warm hands of the corpse, and felt that the warmth of a Martin de Porres was something which the grave could not kill. They went away feeling that his hand was raised in blessing over them.

In the midst of all this, a miracle occurred which caused a tremendous wave of religious enthusiasm to sweep through the town. A noble Spanish lady, Doña Catherine Gonzalez, had been afflicted with a withered arm for twelve years. When she heard of Br. Martin's death and of the miracle of the warmth, she was inspired with a hope that perhaps he might cure her if she could but touch the withered arm to the hand that had lavished so much charity during life.

She made her way to Santo Domingo, and joined the long line of people moving towards the body. Enthusiasm was now very high. Several times already, Doña Catherine heard it whispered, the prior had had to have the habit changed on the corpse because of the number of people who were cutting off pieces to keep as relics.

Doña Catherine was preparing to pour out her whole soul in fervent prayer when her turn came to kneel by the body. But one look at the heavenly charity in that face, and she forgot her prayer, so carefully prepared, to speak simply to him.

"Oh, Br. Martin, please," she said, as she uncovered her arm and moved it slowly across his hand. . . . The tingle of the blood suddenly coursing through her arm made her cry out in surprise and joy. As she sank to her knees by the body her cry of joy was taken up with a tremendous enthusiasm in thousands of souls.

The body of Blessed Martin de Porres was carried to the grave, not by the four lay brothers deputed by the prior, but by an archbishop, a future bishop, a viceroy and a judge of the royal court.

A huge crowd of people followed the remains of a little Black against whose charity dust and the grave had been powerless. Great waves of enchanted prayer beat on the moving crowd.

"He has put down the mighty from their seat and has exalted the humble. . . ."

Seldom in the history of the world have these words been sung with such inspiring truth. For they were burying a man whose every heart-beat had been the heart-beat of a child.

Epilogue

MARTIN DE PORRES AND TODAY

When we look around our modern stone and steel jungles that we call cities, and when we consider the sophistication and complexity of the life led in them, it becomes increasingly obvious that the saint we need is one whose whole soul, to the last fibre of its being, is a contradiction and a challenge to our age.

Ours is a sophisticated age. What passes for Christianity in the neo-pagan atmosphere of today is a heap of dried leaves gathered together in sentiment and nostalgia: so that a poet who voices his age, can face up in the final analysis to the great Mystery of the Incarnation with a bankruptcy of soul:

". . . Once again,
As in previous years we have seen the actual Vision and failed
To do more than entertain it as an agreeable
Possibility, once more we have sent Him away,
Begging though to remain His disobedient servant."

There is a dryness of soul in these lines from Auden's "At the Manger," which sends a shiver of horror through us as we think of all that is implied in them. For they are the human voice crying in its own wilderness — a wilderness created in human souls by the evaporation of the heavenly, earth-softening dew that is the Mystery of a God Made Man.

Our age is also a shallow one, and sophisticated shallowness is the shallowest of all. And the analysis of the sophisticated and right-up-to-date soul gives very often an inventory which is equivalent in its terms to the contents of the bins on our streets.

So we become blasé and bored — we even dream that we are bored, in a refinement of boredom: for all the songs have been left unsung and all the books unread.

It is in the midst of all this that a great wave of devotion began, and spread rapidly, to Blessed Martin de Porres who had been beatified in 1837.

In 1935, this devotion gave rise to the "Blessed Martin Guild," to honor the great American Apostle of Charity and to promote his canonization. His shrine — which became the world center of the devotion — is in Union City, New Jersey: so that the heart of this devotion is challengingly placed in the very heart of the sophisticated world.

In the midst of the celebrations for the third centenary of Blessed Martin's death (1939), Peru named him its patron of Social Justice — "Since, because of his parentage, and his charity for unfortunates of all classes he is the symbol of interracial fraternity and class solidarity, the two great foundations of national unity; we decree that Blessed Martin de Porres be considered as patron and special protector of all works of social justice in Peru. . . ."

The canonization of Blessed Martin took place in 1962. It was Pope John XXIII who solemnly and officially proclaimed him to be St. Martin de Porres. Honors are being heaped on the name of the humble little mulatto who considered himself the servant of all.

We need St. Martin de Porres today. We need his humility, his charity, his childlike simplicity. We have the chill of the West in our soul, and our dreams and striving are a meaningless tangle.

Martin de Porres comes to us with the East in his eyes, and the freshness of the morning about him, that we may learn again to become as little children.

III

BENEDICT THE BLACK

(Translated by Malachy Carroll from the French of Pol de Léon Albaret O.F.M., originally published by Editions Franciscaines, Paris)

INTRODUCTION

I had come to Sicily in search of a man called Benedict the Black.

I was searching for a man who died about four hundred years ago and whose memory has gradually faded from men's minds. I wanted to do something to remedy this, for I was absolutely convinced that Benedict the Black has an important message for the present generation. This had led me that morning to Sicily: I was determined to call him, as it were, from that glass tomb in which he has reposed, an enigmatic smile on his lips, for four centuries.

Some might regard my journey as a somewhat quixotic one, but for me it was a quest with real and exciting perspectives which made it well worth the trouble.

When I was pursuing my clerical studies, and gradually becoming acquainted through the breviary with the saints of my Order, I found my curiosity aroused by the one called St. Benedict the Moor, whose black skin and cultural heritage made him stand out from the others.

The few lines in the lessons of the second nocturn presented him as picturesquely as one could wish, among the gallery of original figures who compose the golden Franciscan Legend. He remained, however, somewhat of a vague impression at the back of my mind.

But that was before I went to Africa. There, contact with his black brothers made me keenly interested in the saint whom today we would call Benedict the Black.

An encounter in a museum at Valladolid led to the respect and love of friendship rather than to mere acquaintance. In one of the treasure-filled rooms, a big wooden statue stood in many-colored splendor. The figure represented a black Franciscan, and that Franciscan was undoubtedly Benedict! I stood there for a long time, contemplating that extraordinary face full of intelligence, of vivacity, of that goodness to which the saints alone attain.

The warmth of my feeling made me want to know Benedict better and everything I discovered about him filled me with admiration. I resolved that I would attempt to take from the shadow of oblivion, especially for the benefit of my black friends, this truly beautiful black man. His brothers can well be proud of this great African, and turn to him for assistance in this magnificent, but difficult, period when they are taking their destiny into their own hands.

But the life of Benedict is of interest to others besides Blacks. His extraordinary virtues offer a particularly opportune example to the men of this age. It is my ardent wish that this short account may multiply the friends of St. Benedict the Black throughout the world, and may communicate to them his God-given message for mankind — a message with special relevance to our own times.

1. A LITTLE SICILIAN VILLAGE

Vincenzo Manasseri's house was among the most prominent in the village of San Filadelfo. (The name has been changed to San Fratello, through the love of the inhabitants for St. Benedict, the little black Friar [Fratello] who was born there.) At the center of a big, sprawling farm, were the squat buildings in which the master and his family lived, while to right and left stretched the stables, the outhouses, the barns.

The village is perched on the slope of a mountain. As the crow flies, it is about six miles from the sea, but about eight miles by the bad road which snakes its way up the mountain through the dips and around the crags. It is part of the diocese of Messina, but is almost equidistant from that city and from Palermo.

Manasseri was a rich man, a careful man who had used his fortune so that it increased and multiplied. He was so rich that he could afford to purchase slaves — Blacks so unfortunate as to be seized in raids on the African coasts and brought like cattle into Europe. But at least it could be said in Manasseri's favor that he treated his slaves well, by the standard of those times — the sixteenth century — and was among the best of the slave-owners. Indeed, he confided the overseeing of his slaves and the responsibility for the cultivation of his lands to one of these very slaves, whose name was Christopher.

143

We know nothing about this Christopher and his wife Diana Larcan, except that their parents were slaves and therefore they were born into slavery. The documents of Benedict's process of canonization refer to them as "Ethiopians," but in the sixteenth century this was the general name used for all black people.

We can safely conclude from the color of their skin and from the fact that they were born in Sicily of slave parents, that these parents had been snatched from the African coasts, the only regions in which at that time the slave-traders sought their unfortunate merchandise.

In the early part of the sixteenth century, Sicily was under the domination of the House of Aragon. The Spanish and the Portuguese were the chief suppliers of slaves to the Christian world. We may surmise that some time between 1450 and 1480, one of their ships had carried to the Sicilian markets a few hundred of these poor captives, exhausted by a brutish voyage in the stench-filled holds of the ship. The chroniclers of the period tell us that often only one tenth of the captives finished such horrible journeys alive. Among the survivors of one such journey were the parents of Christopher and of his wife Diana.

Their children were baptized and brought up in the Catholic religion. Conversions among such captives occurred in a situation which allowed very little freedom of choice. To justify their cruel behavior, the slave-traders and those who profited by their crimes, silenced any uneasiness of conscience by claiming that, for the Africans, loss of liberty was fully compensated for by the salvation of their souls!

Christopher was a man of great integrity, respected for his honesty and his religious outlook, and also for his intelligence. His master was quick to notice these qualities, and gave Christopher a free hand in the administration of his possessions and the direction of his household affairs. This appointment certainly showed how highly his master esteemed him.

In Christopher, there was no hint of resentment towards this man who exercised over him the right of life and death. He even took his master's name, for the historians refer to him as Christopher Manasseri. This indicates an attitude of affection towards Manasseri, whom he must have come to look upon as a father.

In spite of this, however, we are happy to note in both Christopher and his wife a refusal to accept their condition. They could have lived in passive resignation, or, worse still, with a kind of brutish insensitivity which would have put them actually at the animal level. The law was a cruel one: the children of slaves were themselves born into slavery. Rather than bring slaves into the world, Christopher and Diana decided that they would have no children.

The desire of the black man in captivity to perpetuate himself is no recent phenomenon, and in Africa, childless marriages have dim prospects even in the face of religious sanctions. This decision therefore is mute evidence of a desperate response to an impossible situation.

When he heard about this, Manasseri promised that he would emancipate their first child. This was a generous act on his part. So it came about that, in the year 1526, a son was born to Christopher and Diana. We cannot be more precise about the date, since the baptismal registers of San Filadelfo have been lost.

The child was christened Benedict, in Latin, Benedictus, the blessed one. This dark-skinned child was to have an extraordinary destiny which would make him indeed blessed of men, blessed of God.

2. "GO, SELL YOUR OXEN"

We know very little about the infancy of Benedict. He grew up with his parents, and led the life of all those Sicilian children one sees running around in the streets, for Sicily has changed very little. They are cheerful and laughing, but grown-up life has already cast its shadow upon them: so one also sees them solemnly leading their donkey and cart, or helping their parents at work.

Benedict's race, however, would have made a difference between him and his little companions, and the color of his skin and his African traits must often have singled him out for their thoughtless but hurtful teasings. This was probably all the worse due to the fact that be showed a greater inclination towards prayer than towards play.

Father John of Capistrano, who, in 1808, wrote the life of St. Benedict, presents him as already at this age amazing his family and neighbors by his piety. We distrust the efforts of those who seek at all costs to find extraordinary signs in the childhood of those who were destined to great holiness. Saints do not come ready made into the world. Their sanctity is won through ceaseless efforts to perfect their characters in accordance with the Christian ideal. Strength of will and divine grace, rather than natural endowment are the ingredients of sanctity. In a less

147

sensational way, the sources for the life of St. Benedict reveal him as having been a precociously mature child, loving the things of God, devoted to prayer.

As a boy, Benedict used to be sent out to watch over the pasturing animals. Early every morning, he would drive out to the fields his flock of animals, his cows and his sheep; they would move along, and with them a cloud of dust. In the evening, he would drive them home again, to be watered and shut up in the sheds. Always, the wolves roamed around, ever ready to pounce on any animal that strayed.

Like every other child of his condition, Benedict did not go to school. Though intelligent and alert, he was nevertheless to remain illiterate. The Bull of Canonization stresses this fact. It is scarcely surprising: at that time, only those destined for Holy Orders and the children of the rich went to school, the education they received being anyhow of a pretty scanty nature.

When the boy reached the age of ten years, Vicenzo Manasseri kept the promise he had made to Christopher and Diana at the outset of their marriage. In full and legal fashion, he emancipated Benedict, thus ending his slave status.

Since they were slaves, Christopher and Diana had no possessions. They were part of the goods and chattels of their master. If this master chose to give them some gifts, he could always take them back. But this was not now the situation in the case of Benedict. He was able to save up what little money he earned, with the result that, at the age of eighteen, he had enough to buy a pair of oxen and to hire himself out for work in the fields. He gave to the poor the greater part of the money he made in this way.

What set Benedict the boy apart from his companions, made Benedict the young man even more dissimilar to his adolescent companions. They resented the fact that he did not behave like them, and that he was untainted by their vices. They therefore took every opportunity to revenge themselves on him because his way of life was a silent condemnation of theirs.

His slave origins and the color of his skin were obvious targets for their sarcasm. One day, during a work break, they became so exasperated by his calm and by his smiling self-mastery, that they set up a real chorus of jeers and sneers. Their "smart" and cutting remarks were beating on him like hail, when one of the nobility of Sicily passed by. This was Jerome Lanza who, "urged by the Spirit of God," had retired with a few companions to a place of solitude not far from San Filadelfo.

Jerome Lanza was highly impressed by the serenity of this young man, who was behaving with such dignity in the midst of all these provocations. With a sensitivity and insight truly amazing in retrospect, he turned to Benedict's insulting companions and said to them:

"You are now mocking this poor Black, but very soon you will be astounded at the renown he will gain."

Then, addressing the works overseer, he said:

"Take good care of that young man. In a short time, he will come to me to be one of my hermits."

Benedict became very thoughtful when he heard this. He was seeking his way, in silence and in prayer. What the hermit said provided a first suggestion of what that way should be. After that, he redoubled his prayers, asking God to show him His will. One day, during his twenty-first year, when he was leading his oxen over the plain, he met Jerome Lanza.

"What are you doing, Benedict?" he said. "Sell your oxen, give the money to the poor, and come to the hermitage with me."

Benedict heard this as a clear call from God, a call which he must obey, and that immediately. He had become very fond of his oxen, the companions of all his working hours. They were all that he had, and he must sell them to answer the call.

The Apostles, at the Master's call, abandoned their boats and their nets by which they earned their living. This was the most eloquent act of faith they could make in Him who had called them. To renounce his oxen was, for Benedict, an act as heroic as that of the Apostles.

When we read such episodes in the lives of the saints, we tend to regard them as minor events, the important events being what come afterwards.

For my part, I linger in wonder over the heroic quality of this young African's love of God — a love which led him to cut himself off from the whole pattern of his former life, and to throw himself into a great spiritual adventure.

The Gospel tells us about a certain young man "with great possessions" whom Jesus called to follow Him. But he could not face up to being without them, and therefore he is not among the disciples whom we venerate today. Benedict's pair of oxen meant even more to him than did the lands and houses and money transactions to that rich young man whom Jesus loved and who turned away from the love offered to him. They were his foothold on freedom.

Everyone is similarly faced with certain choices which decide the whole pattern of his life. As the poet John Oxenham said, "to every man, there openeth a way, and ways, and a Way." Benedict was about to enter on the rugged Way which would lead to the heights of holiness.

3. THE HERMITS OF THE MOUNTAIN

Following the coast road from Palermo, you turn right to get to San Filadelfo. Some eight miles of winding road raise you to an altitude of 2,000 feet. The countryside is very impressive, dominated by bare mountains. When you reach the first houses, you see a high stony mass which dwarfs the buildings at its foot.

Nothing now exists of the sixteenth century village. All the houses have gone, destroyed by successive earth tremors, and have been replaced by the present, relatively recent ones. The parish church which Benedict frequented is no longer there, but another church stands on its exact site. On the right flank of this church is an old Franciscan friary, built there after Benedict's death in homage to his holiness. You can still admire the fine cloister, but it is no longer occupied by Franciscan friars. The cells have been converted into homes, and the cloister rings with the noise of playing children.

We can easily imagine what life must have been like in that tiny village closed in on itself, imprisoned by the surrounding mountains, and isolated by the considerable distances which lay between it and the nearest villages. The nearest, on the coast, was Santa Agata de Militello, some nine and a half miles away. With

151

the rudimentary means of transport at that time, such a journey would be a severe one, made hazardous by the fact that you might be attacked by bandits, or have the misfortune to meet with a pack of hungry wolves or with some other wild beasts. Dealing with Benedict's life as a hermit, his first biographers stress the "ferrarum pericula" — the dangers from wild beasts.

The village, therefore, lived its life very much within its own limits. News from the outside world came rarely. One of the special subjects of conversation among the villagers was Jerome Lanza, for he was indeed a singular young man. He was rich, of noble lineage, and related to celebrated people such as Cardinal Rabiba. He had everything needed to carve for himself a brilliant career in the world. He married, but on the day of his marriage he suggested to his wife that they should live a life of single chastity, and she agreed. Shortly afterwards, with his wife's consent, he entered a Franciscan friary, where he made his profession of the three vows of poverty, chastity, and obedience.

Jerome Lanza was certainly an eccentric of a restless and perhaps somewhat unstable temperament. No sooner was he married than he began to think about entering the religious life; and just as he had soon left his wife, he also soon left the friary to live in a remote place, with some companions, as a hermit. Perhaps one so eccentric as he could have found final satisfaction only in the individualistic life of the hermit. There is an old proverb which says that "God sometimes writes straight with crooked lines." He makes use of all sorts of things, even of natural defects, to draw souls to Himself.

Jerome had chosen for his life of silence one of those solitary places which the mountains offer abundantly. It was about two and a half miles from San Filadelfo, near enough for the procuring of what was needed, and far enough away to discourage the noisy gapers. He had built there a hut made of tree boughs as a shelter and as a protection against wild animals.

Very soon he was joined by others, among them some professed members of the Dominican Order. Together they formed a small community of hermits. At the suggestion of Jerome, their leader, who had been a professed member of the Franciscan Order, they placed themselves under the protection of St. Francis of Assisi. The pope had authorized this initiative and had approved the rule which the hermits wished to follow.

In fact, nearly everywhere, under the inspiration of the Holy Spirit and in reaction against the impiety of the age, such eremitical groups were developing. There was a lot of talk in San Filadelfo about the incredible austerities of these men of God living in the mountain nearby. When any one of them came into the village to get the rough food with which they were content, he was watched with awe and reverence.

Persuaded by Jerome, Benedict, having sold his oxen and distributed the money to the poor, went to join the Hermits of St. Francis who were living their mortified and silent life in the impressive mountain solitude. He was then twenty-one years old.

From the outset, he enthusiastically embraced the life of mortification, endeavoring to make yet more harsh the way of life he had hitherto followed. That way of life had by no means been a soft one. There was a grim mortification of its own in the life of a Sicilian farm-worker who, on poor and meagre food, had been accustomed to work hard from dawn to dusk.

Even the normal austerities of the hermits were not enough for Benedict. He immediately adopted habits of an extremely severe kind, and kept them up all his life. He never ate meat, drank the least possible quantity of wine, and was content with one meal once a day of bread and vegetables, just sufficient to prevent starvation. To all this he added hair-shirts and frequent scourging even to blood. Exhausted by prayer, he slept only a few hours a night, lying on the ground.

This severe life had nothing in common with that of a fakir eager to seek out ever new ascetic practices. His mind was ceaselessly fixed on the divine countenance of Jesus. It was the Christ of sorrows suffering for the sins of man, who had invited him into this way of penance. Often, Jerome Lanza found it necessary to restrain the ardor of this novice, thus preventing him from completely undermining his health.

After five years of probation, Benedict was allowed to take his solemn (i.e. perpetual) vows. By his heroic virtue — as Pope Pius VII tells us in the Bull of Canonization — he surpassed all his companions in fervor and in austerity of life.

Already highly curious about everything concerning the community of hermits, the villagers were made even more so by the fact that Benedict, one of their "own," was now a member. When they met together after the day's work, they would talk about the life of terrible austerity which was being led by him whom already they were beginning to call "the Black Saint." All the more so, since God Himself was pleased to manifest, by miracles, the holiness of Benedict.

A sick villager had come to ask Benedict to pray for him, and Benedict had done so immediately. The sick person was cured on the spot. The news spread like wild fire from the village to the neighboring hamlets. Very soon, all the sick people of the whole area were making their way to the hermitage, hoping that Benedict would cure them.

In greater and greater numbers, they came to ask for prayers, to tell their sufferings, to demand miracles. The few miles which, at the outset, protected the hermits, were now regarded as just a walking distance for all those who were eager to see the Black Saint, and to benefit by his influence with God.

The Sicilian crowd is a highly excitable one. A familiarity with God and His servants gives to it's displays of piety a picturesque and colorful character. I can recall a typical instance of this at the Franciscan Church of Santa Maria di Gesù in Palermo. A pious woman was demanding, in a loud voice, that the Father Guardian should allot to her intention a Mass for a date she had chosen:

"You can't refuse me, Reverendo," she pleaded. "It is not I who am asking you, but the dead woman for whom the Mass will be celebrated!"

The hermitage was becoming a place of popular pilgrimage, and of Sicilian pilgrimage at that! From dawn to dusk, and sometimes late into the night, the place was loud with the noise of supplications, of prayers recited in a loud voice, of the groanings of the sick, mixed with the unspiritual wranglings (one remembers the like in connection with Padre Pio) of those disputing places in the queue.

The solitaries withdrew as much as they could from this invasion, trying to safeguard a little of their silent communing with God. But the crowd made their way into the huts and the places of prayer, demanding Benedict and threatening to bring him by force to where the sick were lying on the ground.

Life became insupportable, and the only solution was flight. One night, the hermits packed their few belongings and stole away to a more solitary place called la Platanella.

The following day, there was consternation among the pilgrims who found only empty huts awaiting them. They set off in search of the hermits, and of course found them. This was only the first of a number of such flights by Jerome Lanza and his disciples to escape from this excessive devotion, until finally they came to Monte Pellegrino, about six miles from Palermo. There they found the equivalent in solitude, though of a more rugged character, to what they had lost by leaving San Filadelfo.

Ten years had passed since Benedict left his native village and his family to answer the call of God. The fervor he had shown in the early stages was no straw fire: it increased and deepened. Under the influence of the Holy Spirit, he had reached greater heights of self-detachment in order to allow himself to be taken over fully by God whom he hungrily sought in constant prayer.

The group of hermits to which he belonged had increased. Jerome Lanza, who had remained its father and head, died, worn out by austerities, leaving his community in some confusion.

Someone had to take his place. The hermits consulted together and their unanimous choice was Benedict. We may be sure that it was not the austerity of his life nor his reputation for holiness which alone led them to this decision. A man can be truly master of himself and a wonder-working saint, and yet lack the qualities essential to a good superior. Among the most important of such qualities are good sense and judgment, a love of his brethren which gives him a sympathetic attitude towards them, firmness allied with kindness, a sense of duty which faces up squarely to responsibilities. Men who live together for years can size up one another without delusions of any kind. The appointing of a head was a very serious matter, but the hermits had no hesitation in agreeing that Benedict had all the requisite qualities.

Benedict was most distressed at their choice, and he pleaded against it. What — had they forgotten that he was the son of slave parents, and illiterate? Surely they could not think of placing *him* in charge of a community where so many excelled him in virtue and knowledge! But he pleaded in vain: he had to accept. Thus, at thirty-one years of age, Benedict became the father and head of the Hermits of St. Francis.

Under his paternal direction, the little community continued to live in the silence of Monte Pellegrino. But suddenly something occurred which was to shatter the whole pattern of their existence.

The one thing sought by the Hermits of Monte Pellegrino was that they should be left in peace to lead their life of silence, of simplicity, of penitence. But, alas, they could not hope for blessed obscurity. Their reputation for holiness, and the new miracles wrought by Benedict, had drawn attention to them. The viceroy of Sicily, Giovanni Lacerda, and his wife, had become their friends, and had built for them a little chapel close to the grotto of St. Rosalia, a place of pilgrimage famous throughout Sicily.

This aroused jealousy and hostility from a quarter from which Pascal's aphorism might lead us to expect it: "Evil is never done so fully and so zestfully as when done in the name of conscience." Certain religious, disturbed by the hermits' reputation for holiness, went to Rome and set about persuading Pope Pius IV not to allow the little community to develop any further. The Church, they said, had enough religious orders; there was no need to create new ones. This community which was growing and which enjoyed the patronage of the great, would ultimately become such an order. Certain false insinuations added to these apparently disinterested considerations ended by convincing the pope. In 1562, he reached a decision which meant the end of the Hermits of St. Francis. One day a representative of the archbishop of Palermo came to Monte Pellegrino to convey to Benedict the papal decision and to leave with him a copy of the decree signifying that decision. It declared that the hermits were dispensed from their fourth vow to observe a religious fast; they were to disband, and each of them was to enter some already existent order approved by the Church.

Cold with amazement, Benedict said nothing. He just bowed his head as his sign of assent, and the visitor felt great pity for him. After his departure, Benedict spent a long time in prayer in the little chapel of the hermitage. Then he assembled his brethren and told them about the pontifical decree. As he spoke, consternation gripped all the religious. There was nothing, they thought, to justify a decision so brutal and with all the signs of an injustice. Besides, their own whole future was at stake.

These men, who held one another in affection and esteem, must submit to painful separation. What was being offered to them in exchange for their beloved solitude, for their life of silence and of austerity? Entry into large monasteries amid the tumult of towns and cities, with numerous religious in conditions totally unlike those they had for long years been accustomed to. This was indeed a superhuman trial.

There must have been a great temptation to complain, perhaps to revolt, anyhow to go to Rome to seek a reversal of the decision. Yet not for one instant did Benedict hesitate. The will of God was manifested by this order from the pope, and for Benedict that was that. His acceptance was nonetheless an agonizing one: for the second time, Benedict was at the hour of anguished choice.

4. AN ANGUISHED CHOICE

Benedict was the head of his community. He had exhorted them to obedience, and now he must show an immediate example to his brethren. Without delay, he began to seek out the religious family which would best suit his temperament and his original vocation. Already a son of St. Francis, it was very natural that he should turn his thoughts to the Franciscan family of religious, and equally natural that he should think particularly about the Capuchins. The latter were still very close to their origins, and were endeavoring to lead the eremitical life.

However, Benedict wanted to have God's approval for his choice. He went to the cathedral of Palermo, and there, before a statue of the Blessed Virgin, he pleaded long with the Lord, through the intercession of Mary, to show him his way. He had made the sacrifice, and there was no going back, but which of the ways ahead was to be chosen?

It is easy to envisage this scene in the great cathedral of Palermo. We can picture this African of thirty-six, prostrate before the statue of the Madonna. People must have turned to look at the unusual sight of this dark-skinned religious praying with such fervor. But Benedict, absorbed in his prayer, was wholly unconscious of the curiosity he was awakening.

"Lord, tell me, do you really want me to join the Friars Minor

159

Capuchin? Is that really what you want, Lord?"

Three times, the Bull of Canonization tells us, God answered him, and this by a celestial light. What form did this illumination take? The saints have their secrets, and when they choose to keep these secrets to themselves, it is not for us to pry into them.

The answer was clear: yes, Benedict was to join one of the Franciscan families, but not that of the Capuchins. He was to choose that of the Friars Minor of the Observance. This is not the place to recount the history of the various reforms which occurred in the Franciscan Order, under the impulse of events and at the instigation of men of God who desired to see their religious family ever more faithful to the purity of its original vocation.

Pope Leo XIII reunified the great Franciscan Order by suppressing the reforms which, in the course of centuries, had arisen within the ranks of the Observants. Since then, there are only three families of St. Francis: The Franciscans, the Conventuals, and the Capuchins.

Enlightened by God, Benedict went to the Friary of Santa Maria di Gesù, some three and a half miles from Palermo. This friary had been founded by the Blessed Matthew, Bishop of Girgenti, who returned to die there. The conventual church still piously conserves the remains of this man of great virtue.

Benedict asked to be received by the Father Provincial, and then made his request to be accepted as a Friar Minor. Admission into a religious order always raises delicate problems for a superior. In the person's own interests, as well as in those of the order, no mistake must be made. When the postulant is someone as decidedly original in temperament as was Benedict, the provincial must give greater thought to the matter than in the case of some more ordinary person.

This particular provincial was dealing with a man of thirty-six, a former slave, a man with a cultural heritage different from that of the other religious, one who had already sixteen years' experience of the religious life, including several years as superior. How would he fare? Might he not try to impose his own views about the religious life, rather than humbly accept the usages and customs he found in existence? Having become accustomed to exercising authority, could he bring himself to obey as must all the friars?

When he questioned Benedict, the Father Provincial soon realized that he was dealing with an extraordinary man. Benedict's attitude, the clarity and the depth of the answers he gave, were his most eloquent advocates. Furthermore, his reputation for great holiness weighed heavily in his favor. To the great joy of the community, Benedict was admitted as a lay brother. Since he was already a perpetually professed member of the order, he did not have to remain a novice for another year, and so he began immediately to live under the authority of the superior of Santa Maria di Gesù. Some days later, he was sent to the Friary of Santa Anna di Giuliana.

The religious orders are schools of perfection. They are the concrete expression of men's living answer to the call to the perfect life addressed to them by God. "If you seek perfection, go sell your possessions, and give to the poor and follow me," said Christ to the rich young man.

The essence of the religious life is the imitation of the life of Christ, in poverty, obedience, and chastity. Those who answer the call divide their time between prayer and work. This work is specified by the nature of each order.

But the religious life does not necessarily imply ordination to the priesthood for everyone who enters into it. In the orders known as "active," such as the Order of Friars Minor, certain friars — in accordance with their aptitudes and with the studies they have made — will be ordained priests and will devote themselves to the ministry; while others, the lay brothers (known as *conversi*), will occupy their time with prayer and with work useful to the community. On the plane of the religious life, they are the equals of the members who are priests. There are at present (1974) over five thousand lay brothers in the Order of Friars Minor. In the course of the centuries, many such lay brothers have been canonized by the Church.

It will be remembered that Benedict was illiterate. This was an obstacle to his becoming a priest, since to do so would have meant long years devoted to the study of Latin, of philosophy, and of theology. However, knowing his humility, his love of silence and of prayer, we are sure that he would anyhow have asked to be received as a lay brother, even if his early training has been an adequate preparation for the priesthood.

At the Friary of Santa Anna di Giuliana, Benedict began his apprenticeship for his new life. It was a small house of recollection, of the cenobitical life, a kind of hermitage whose friars did no work outside the friary, but devoted themselves there to prayer and to manual labor. In short, it provided a kind of life little different from that which Benedict had hitherto been living. It was a happy transition to what was to follow. There he spent three years about which his biographers tell us very little.

What preceded, as well as what followed, enables us to conjecture what his life was like during those three years. Relieved of the burden of authority, and having no responsibility other than that of self-sanctification, he was able to lead to the full his life of prayer and of penitence. Prayer would urge him to penitence, and penitence would itself become a spring of prayer.

His principal subject of meditation was the Passion of the Lord. He immersed himself in this subject, for there he found the proof of the love which God has for us. As a true son of St. Francis, his constant source of contemplation was Jesus. He used to seek Him in the tabernacle of the church where he would spend a part of his night.

For Benedict, work was the best form of poverty. No task was too mean for him; in fact, he deliberately took on those jobs which the others tended to avoid. Benedict, the solid farm-worker, was the mainstay of the hermitage.

Happy indeed the superiors of such religious! Benedict's Father Guardian did not even need to give an order, for Benedict had divined and fulfilled his wishes even before he had expressed them. Benedict was drawn to God's service by love of Christ. For him, obedience was simply an exquisite form of love. Therefore, he set no reserves to his obedience.

Stories of prodigies occurring during this period have come down to us — eloquent witness to his fellow friars' conviction that God would refuse the servant nothing. One day, there was a shortage of wood for the kitchen fire. In the nearby forest, a tree, struck by lightning, lay on the ground. Having made the Sign of the Cross, Benedict unhesitatingly raised it to his shoulder and carried it to the friary. Ten men together could not have shifted it.

He was very happy in this hermitage of Santa Anna di Giuliana. His sole desire was to pass his whole life there, for there he had found what we had come to seek in the religious life: silence, penitence, unbroken colloquy with God. But the Lord had other ideas for him.

5. A MOST UNUSUAL COOK

Three years of peaceful life had passed at Santa Anna since Benedict had left Monte Pellegrino. Then, one morning in 1567, he received through his superior a message from the Father Provincial. Benedict was to be transferred to the Friary of Santa Maria di Gesù at Palermo.

St. Francis required his sons to live in this world as "pilgrims and strangers," as men of no fixed abode, as nomads on the road. Naturally and understandably, Benedict would have liked to pass the rest of his life at Santa Anna. Had he not re-discovered there the treasures which led him to leave San Filadelfo so many years ago — the treasures of silence, of solitude, of the ascetic life? But such stability would not have been in keeping with his vocation of pilgrim and stranger. Once more, he had to set out and face the unknown.

Why this summons from the Father Provincial to the major Friary of Santa Maria di Gesù? We have no information about this, but we can conjecture that they needed another worker there. Such a need might have arisen through one friar becoming sick; if there had been no one to take his place in Santa Maria, a friar would have had to be transferred from another friary. Perhaps in this case it was the cook, since Benedict was immediately assigned to the kitchen.

Was he able to cook? Italian cooking is not of a complicated kind, and that of the friary would have been even less so. The preparation of pasta dishes is the predominant factor. There is an old joke that just as a duckling knows how to swim the moment it emerges from the egg, so too the Italian is born knowing how to prepare pasta dishes!

Benedict made up for what he lacked in skill by great good will. We have seen that he was both intelligent and obedient. Very quickly, he acquired the knowledge needed for his new task and the community had no reason to regret the provincial's choice.

However, this cook was not like the others. While doing his job to the utmost of his ability, he gave the impression that he was in such close union with God as to be always on the edge of ecstasy. Sometimes, a friar would come to the kitchen to ask a favor, and Benedict would oblige him with great readiness. But if he lingered on to have a chat, Benedict answered evasively and vaguely, so that the subject was soon dropped and the friar went his way. It takes two to make a conversation, and Benedict developed great skill in kindly yet effectively defending his solitude and his silence.

The love of God is inseparable from the love of one's neighbor. Benedict was fully aware of the importance of his new task. He himself practiced very severe penance, but he knew that he had not been sent to the kitchen to make others do so. He carefully prepared for each what his health required, and substantial meals for all as well cooked as he could make them.

By tradition, the cook can allow himself certain little extras, and no one objects, since in his case too the Scriptural text applies: "You shall not muzzle an ox when it is treading out grain." But far from availing himself of such a privilege, Benedict denied himself even what would be regarded as necessary. He never drank wine or ate meat, but kept strictly to bread and vegetables. Throughout the whole year he allowed himself no exception to this rule which he had imposed on himself when he first entered the religious life.

The community was already aware of Benedict's holiness. In

addition, certain mysterious things occurred which centered the friars' attention even more on this strange cook.

Santa Maria di Gesù was an important friary. The provincial chapter — that is, the triennial assembly of the superiors of the province — was usually held there. Once, when they were all gathered there, the provisions began to run short. Snow had settled so thickly that the friars could not go out, as usual, to get help from their benefactors. The reserves were used up and the next day there would be nothing to give to the friars. Though the cook's job was to prepare the food brought to him, not to seek out those provisions, there was nothing against Benedict praying. His trust in God was always unshakable, and once more the Father of the poor would answer his prayer. Of that he was serenely sure.

After Matins in choir, the community settled for the night. Benedict, as usual, remained in the chapel for a long time. Then, inspired by God, he went back to the kitchen, where he filled every pot he could find with water, after which he went to his cell for a few hours' sleep on the floor.

Next day, before dawn had tinted the mountains around Palermo, Benedict went to his kitchen, where to his great joy unusual sounds greeted him. From every pot came the noise of rippling water, and looking in, Benedict saw that God had filled them with fish. Through Benedict's holiness and serene trust in God, the community enjoyed a fine meal.

There was also the occasion when the apostolic inquisitor for the kingdom of Sicily, later archbishop of Palermo, visited the friary. His name was Don Diego d'Ahedo, and he had a great affection for the community. It was Christmas, and he had invited himself for the celebrations. In deference to the poverty of the community, he had sent ample provisions which the cook was to prepare.

Benedict, apparently unconcerned about the important guest whom Providence had confided to him, passed the whole night in prayer, savoring, like his Father, St. Francis, the meekness and humility of the Christ Child in the manger. His ecstatic prayer continued throughout the whole morning, while the kitchen stood empty and silent.

In the Franciscan friaries, at this time, it was usually the Father Vicar who was in charge of material matters. This was an important occasion for the community, with such a guest, and so the Father Vicar went to see how things were getting on in the kitchen. Imagine his astonishment when he got there! The provisions sent by the inquisitor, the fish, the poultry, even a calf, were lying there just as they had arrived, and the fires were just dead ashes.

There was an immediate and urgent search for Benedict, but he was nowhere to be found. The honor of the community was at stake, and the Father Vicar was tormented by the idea of the meal which would have to be served to the inquisitor, a meal richer in excuses and apologies than in food! Meantime, the friars were continuing to search every part of the house, while others were looking in the mountain overhanging the friary, where Benedict had a habit of retiring when he wanted to give himself to prayer.

The time came for the High Mass celebrated by the inquisitor, and the meal was to follow immediately. We can well imagine that the Father Superior and the Father Vicar were pretty distracted in their prayers by thoughts of all that uncooked food in the kitchen, and by the problem of how they were to explain it. And still, no Benedict!

During the Mass, the friar who was acting as thurifer happened to lean against a piece of hanging tapestry, and felt something unusual behind it. He moved the tapestry a little, and yes, there he was — Benedict in complete ecstasy, more preoccupied with the splendor of God than with the cooking of fish and poultry and a calf! Furtively but very decidedly, the friar shook him to bring him back to reality. Coming to himself, Benedict looked at the friar and smiled, and put his finger on his lips to indicate that the chapel was a place for silence. The friar must have been glowing with exasperation, like his own thurible, when he saw that Benedict had every intention of remaining quietly where he was until the end of the Mass. After that, Benedict went serenely to his kitchen, where he found the Father Vicar so heated that some of the food could have been cooked on him! We have no record of what he said to Benedict, but we can easily imagine it!

Tranquilly, Benedict lit the fire, assuring the Father Vicar that all the community needed to do was to go to the refectory and everything would be ready on time. The Father Vicar looked in silent bewilderment around the kitchen, at the raw fish, the uncooked chickens, the calf still hanging on its hook, the vegetables, the ingredients for the pasta. This was beyond him! He went out of the kitchen!

A few minutes later, he came back to find out how long he had to ask the inquisitor and the community to wait for the meal. The poor man must have nearly burst a blood vessel when he found Benedict on his knees in the middle of the kitchen, his face alight with ecstasy. He shook him violently, and once again Benedict gave him that maddeningly serene smile, and assured him that all the community had to do was to go immediately to the refectory. For what?, the Father Vicar must have asked. To chew raw meat and raw vegetables.

By this time, the friars had come to the kitchen, and were offering suggestions about what could be done. The inquisitor, too, had got wind of it, and he came to the kitchen, highly amused and intrigued by it all. Then, to everyone's astonishment, two young men dressed in white appeared, and, having rolled up their sleeves, began to prepare the meal with superhuman speed and dexterity. Once again, Benedict calmly asked the community to go to the refectory, and this time they did so, like men in a dream. Very soon, delicious dish succeeded delicious dish, to the great comfort and edification of the brethren. The angels had come to Benedict's assistance.

There are other less spectacular and less picturesque wonders recorded of Benedict. They reveal the gift of infused knowledge and the gift of reading hearts by which God manifested His close intimacy with His servant.

Father Vincenzo Magis, a learned Dominican, was a great friend of Benedict. This religious had such a high reputation for learning and virtue that the Holy See named him archbishop of Palermo, but through humility he refused this honor in order to continue to live with his brethren.

One day, saddened at not being able to understand a certain passage of Holy Scripture, he decided to consult Benedict about it. He went to the friary, and as he was asking the porter to send for Benedict, Benedict himself came to the door and greeted him with the words:

"Father, please do not be troubled at not understanding this passage of Holy Scripture. I shall explain it clearly to you."

Then he led the Dominican to his cell and made him sit down beside him. Taking the words one by one, he expounded the passage with such clarity and doctrinal depth that the astounded theologian found all the obscurity melting away like early mist in the sun's rays.

On leaving the friary, Father Magis said to the friars whom he met:

" Fathers, you have here a great saint. Not only did he know without my telling him what I had come to ask him, but he explained with the utmost clarity a very obscure passage of Holy Scripture which was completely puzzling me. Clearly, this man has received from God the gift of infused knowledge."

All these things attracted such attention to Benedict that they led to a further change in his way of life.

6. THE RELUCTANT SUPERIOR

For eleven years, Benedict did the cooking at the Friary of Santa Maria di Gesù, to the satisfaction of all. Once more, he thought he had found his way and he hoped that, for the remainder of his life, he would remain at this humble post.

No doubt, he was very often disturbed in his prayer and his work by the visitors who came to seek his advice, to recommend themselves to his prayers, or to request a miracle. But all this was part of charity to his neighbor, and therefore there was no question of trying to avoid it. During the night, at least, he was free to yield himself to the ecstasy to which he was always liable. At times of ecstasy, his face, emaciated by his severe penances, would become all radiant with the interior splendor of his soul.

Wholly devoted to his work and to his God, Benedict was scarcely affected by the agitation which reigned at that time in the friary. Important changes were under way, changes involving all the friars, at Santa Maria di Gesù. In general assemblies, attended by all the superiors of the province, important decisions had been made.

These decisions concerned, in the first place, the houses. Several friaries of the province were erected into houses of the Franciscan reform or of the recollection (Reformati). Henceforward, in these houses the way of life would have to become more severe, and the rule would have to be more strictly observed. Santa Maria di Gesù was among the friaries chosen.

But the chapter also appointed the Father Guardians of each community. St. Francis had forbidden those of his sons who exercised authority to use the current title of religious superiors. They were not to be called abbot or prior, but simply servant (*minister*) or guardian (*custos*). Among the Franciscans, the superior is the guardian of the soul and body of his brethren.

A Father Guardian had to be assigned to Santa Maria di Gesù. As we know, it was an important friary, with a community containing many priests. Its position as a newly created house of the reform made the post a particularly delicate one. Modifications had to be made in the previous way of life, and new austerities imposed which ran counter to the set ways. Had all the religious been saints, such innovations would have presented no difficulty whatsoever. But men come to the religious life in order to become saints; they are not saints already.

The new Father Guardian of Santa Maria di Gesù would have to expect to meet with opposition. The Sicilian character, excitable and headstrong, would make that opposition still more redoubtable. The provincial superiors had therefore to give long and careful consideration to the matter before appointing the man who would have to bear such a burden. The ways of God are inscrutable: Benedict, the community cook, was elected to be the Father Guardian of Santa Maria di Gesù!

A lay brother as superior of Santa Maria! Had the choice been someone of similar position other than this extraordinary man, it might have seemed a deliberate provocation. Even more than in the miracles and prodigies which marked the life of the humble cook, we can see in this appointment the proclamation of his human qualities and of his supernatural virtues.

Let us remind ourselves that Benedict was the son of slave parents, and himself once a slave. His skin was black, and, as shown by the statues we have of him, his physical traits were those of an African. In this sixteenth century society, so imbued with its intellectual superiority, this alone would have marked Benedict as an object of disdain and condescension. As a slave, he had belonged to someone else, he had had a status little above that of a beast of burden, a past which a society in which slavery still existed let a man rise above only reluctantly and in small steps.

Furthermore, perhaps most serious of all, he was illiterate. He had never attended a school, and he had absolutely nothing of that technical intellectual refinement of which the scholars among his brethren were so proud. The poor man knew no Latin! He spoke the Sicilian language, a hodgepodge of Arabic, Spanish, and Italian words, with some vestiges of French. Even more than his former slave condition and his African origins, this lack of education was a major obstacle to the respect and obedience of his scholarly brethren.

Of course, Benedict had already exercised authority over the little community of the hermits of Jerome Lanza. But the latter were few, and mostly laymen. The position of Santa Maria di Gesù was quite different. As we have already said, the community was a large one, composed principally of priests who were exercising the ministry, and among whom were some professors. Besides these priests, there was a group of novices, educated young men who were continuing their studies in order to become priests. Furthermore, there were the lay brothers, Benedict's working companions. All had known him as the friary cook, and this further complicated an already complex situation. In the Church, as indeed in nearly all institutions, one rarely finds that a leader is chosen from the ranks of those over whom he is to exercise authority. Usually, someone is appointed from outside.

When he heard about this choice, Benedict was absolutely dumbfounded. He hastened to the friary where the superiors were meeting to plead for a reversal of the decision. With tears in his eyes, he urged his incompetence, and his lack of education — why, he could not even read or write! What would be the reaction of all Sicily to this choice? Would they not despise the Franciscans for having placed in charge of an important community of priests, a lay brother, an illiterate man, a former slave, a son of slave parents, a man of black skin?

The provincial fathers were already aware of all this; in fact, it was all this that had motivated their choice. They refused to budge. As always, in such circumstances, they lavished words of encouragement on the poor cook, showing him all the good that was to be done in his new post, and assuring him that he had all the qualities needed for it. They even gave him some advice about the way to govern the community! But when Benedict continued to plead, they reminded him somewhat firmly about his vow of obedience. Benedict had no answer to that: he bowed his head in silent assent, and big tears trickled down his dark cheeks. The reminder about his vow of obedience had killed all resistance in him. He had given himself to God. God was using him in a way he himself would not have chosen, but God was the Master.

Benedict was a man of great moral virtue, but this alone would not have fitted him for his new task had it not been complemented by the human qualities needed in those called upon to lead others. Those qualities can be summed up in the one word, *wisdom.*

Wisdom demands, first of all, the intelligence to judge well any given situation and to find the means suited to deal with it. In the application of those means, prudence is required, for sometimes the remedies turn out worse than the evils they were intended to remedy. It is wisdom which enables a man to adapt to each the general measures decided for all, so that there is no danger of these measures becoming insupportable.

Wisdom is inseparable from kindness and consideration. Laws are made for men, not men for the laws. St. Francis' idea of the guardian was that he should be, first and foremost, a father. Writing to Friar Elias, who had been put at the head of the whole order, he laid down this splendid axiom: "Love, because no man can continue to uphold and sustain where he has ceased to love." The kindness of the father — where it is real kindness and not a misnomer for weakness — is also marked by compassion towards the weaknesses of human nature, towards the sufferings of soul and of body.

Benedict was deeply aware of all this. His years of authority over the hermits had given him some experience of ruling men. Above all, his experience enabled him to appreciate what a delicate and difficult task this was.

The cook, suddenly promoted to the highest place, immediately put into effect the one and only means by which he could secure from others what he demanded of them: he required nothing from them that he did not himself first fulfil to the utmost.

Before dawn, he was in choir, the first to arrive there; every night, when the others had retired to sleep, he was still kneeling in prayer before the tabernacle or before the statue of the Blessed Virgin whom he had chosen as Queen and Mother of his community. Always present at the exercises in choir, he was to all a living model of prayer, or recollection, of modesty.

But the whole day in a friary is not passed in formal prayer. Much work has to be done. That he had become Father Guardian did not mean that Benedict was prepared to give up his beloved manual work. In fact, he seems to have used his new position as an opportunity to extend such activities.

The documents of the process of beatification show him, at this period, working in the kitchen, sweeping the chapel and the corridors, chopping wood, washing linen. Wherever he saw any of his brethren weary or in difficulties, Benedict would go to his assistance. How could one refuse to such a leader whatever he asked?

The upkeep of a community of Franciscans presents complex problems. The rule does not allow any fixed revenue. Everything is put in the hands of Providence. When the friars have labored in ministering or in preaching or in rendering some other service, they can accept, in recompense, whatever is spontaneously offered to them. In no case may they demand a salary. Whatever they receive is brought back to the friary, where everything is in common. Whenever such spontaneous payments for services did not suffice for the daily needs, the lay brothers used to go out collecting alms from door to door. This is what Francis called "resorting to the Lord's table." The fruits of work, the alms received, are still sometimes insufficient. In such cases, it is the Father Guardian, responsible for the life of his brethren, who must provide for the necessities of each.

Benedict was attentive to the material problems of his community. He appreciated that while man should live by the word of God, he must also have a little food. When the food was running short, despite all the normal sources, he did not hesitate to resort to the miraculous.

There was one highly colorful occurrence which clearly shows the extraordinary gifts which Benedict had received from God.

Antonio Vignes was a Catalan merchant living in Palermo. He had chartered a ship at Barcelona, and had it loaded with bales of cloth and with other merchandise to be sold in Sicily. His whole fortune was tied up in that ship. Forty days had passed, and there was no news of it, so that Antonio naturally feared that it had been lost on the high seas or had been captured by pirates. That meant ruin for him and for his family.

Tortured with anxiety, he went to see Benedict, who told him not to fear but to say his prayers; his ship would reach port, safe and sound.

Antonio spent further weary days scanning the horizon, but in vain. He returned to the friary. Benedict again reassured him: his ship had sheltered from bad weather in a Sardinian harbor. While they were talking together, Antonio saw on the skyline a ship in full sail towards Palermo.

"There it is!" he cried.

"No," Benedict answered, "that is a ship from Majorca. Yours will show up very soon."

Sure enough, two days later, Antonio's ship cast anchor at Palermo, having been delayed by contrary winds in a Sardinian harbor.

Antonio Vignes was not an ungrateful man. Some days later, he brought a great quantity of cooked fish, and accompanied by several servants carrying the fish, he set off for Santa Maria di Gesù. He told no one about this, because he wanted to give the friars a pleasant surprise.

On that particular day, provisions had run very low in the friary, and the community were resigned with what little they had. But just as the bell-ringer was about to give the signal for going to the refectory, the Father Guardian told him to wait a while because Antonio Vignes was at that very moment bringing ready-cooked fish. Benedict also told the porter to go to the door to receive the benefactor who would arrive at any moment.

Antonio was amazed to find that he was expected. Having delivered his gift to Benedict, he went away, astounded at the power of the servant of God.

In every friary, a bigger cell is allotted to the Father Guardian, centrally placed in order to be easily accessible to each and all. Benedict had to occupy this cell, but he had all the furniture removed, and was content with what had up to then been given to him: a straw mattress placed on the floor, and a crucifix and some simple pious pictures hanging on the wall.

It was to this poor cell that the friars would come to see their Father Guardian. They always received a warm welcome, especially those whom he felt to be most opposed to his measures of reform.

The religious life is a hard and constant trial. Temptations are not lacking, and discouragement is a frequent danger. When weariness sets in, the religious feel a dry distaste for the burden which has become too heavy. In such circumstances, solitude is a bad counselor.

A Father Guardian must be attentive to these crises which occur among his spiritual sons, so that he may be able to guide and encourage them. Benedict had that paternal solicitude which is always on the alert. But in addition, he was so enlightened by God that he could quickly sense these difficult moments in his spiritual sons. He would call the particular friar and talk to him about God. He would do so in such a natural way, and with such conviction and fervor, that the friar would gradually open his heart to him and confide to him his troubles. As so often in such cases, this would be sufficient to dispel the gloom. Benedict had saved one of his brethren, and won for himself another devoted disiple.

Whenever a miracle was needed to save souls in danger, Benedict would seek it from God. Two religious who were the beneficiaries of one such miracle, have given an account of it during the process of beatification. Fathers Gregory Licata and Jerome di Palermo, when they were as yet novices, were beset by temptation. They confided to each other their distaste for the religious life, and planned to run away together during the night. As novices, they were quite free to leave openly, but no doubt lacked courage to do so. Hence their secret plan.

At three o'clock on a January morning, they scaled the wall, and set off along the road to Palermo. To their utter astonishment, there facing them in the middle of the road was none other than Benedict himself. Affectionately, he reproached them for their lack of generosity. With bowed heads, the two novices accompanied him back to the friary.

Some time later, they made a second, similar attempt at flight. Once again, Benedict was awaiting them on the road. He assured them that he knew that their vocation was to be Friars Minor, and that they were endangering their eternal salvation by attempting to evade it.

Thoroughly convinced this time, the two young men persevered, and later became eminent members of the order. All their lives, they thanked God for having revealed their weakness to Benedict, thus enabling him to save them.

There were also the weak who gave bad example to others by refusing to accept the conventual discipline. Benedict did not capitulate to them. He used to call them to him, and show them how bad for the novices was the example of priests, of erudite religious, who exempted themselves from obedience. Great virtue is needed in a superior to carry out this duty of correction; it is so much easier to let things take their course, but to act in this way is a dereliction of duty rooted in moral cowardice. Benedict fulfilled this duty with such meekness, such charity, such courtesy, that those reprimanded by him felt grateful.

During the three years of Benedict's term of office, the community of Santa Maria di Gesù grew steadily in virtue, so that it became a model friary of the reform. The regular life was exactly observed there, but, still more important, the friary became noted for its atmosphere of exquisite charity. Instead of being self-incapsulated in a kind of spiritual egotism, each friar was concerned about his brother, attentive to his needs, his sufferings, his joys, and a respecter of his intimacy with God. The provincial superiors were proved right: Benedict had succeeded beyond their most optimistic hopes.

7. A COACH OVERTURNED, AND THE DEAD RAISED TO LIFE

We have already seen that Benedict's great desire was to remain until death wherever he was and in the post he was holding. The exception to this was his post as Father Guardian. While fulfilling it to the utmost of his ability and, as we have seen, with great success, his unfailing wish was to lay aside this burden which weighed heavily on him and thus to regain the peace of his beloved solitude.

In 1581, the general meeting of the superiors of the province was held at Girgenti, now called Agrigenti. As a Father Guardian, Benedict had to attend. The population of the little town heard that he was coming, and prepared to give him a triumphal reception. The Sicilian temperament loves this sort of public display, whose purpose is more than merely to honor a servant of God. The news of the wonders performed by the Black Saint had reached Girgenti, and this is not surprising, since people had come from Spain and Portugal to seek his intercession. To have a saint of such stature in their midst was a great event. Perhaps he would give them some display of his power. Everyone had some disease to be cured, some great favor to obtain!

Benedict suffered intensely from these cries of admiration,

these displays of veneration. He pulled his hood over his head, and stuck his hands deeply up his sleeves to prevent the crowd, especially the highly excitable women, from covering them with kisses. During his stay at Girgenti, he devoted himself more than ever to prayer. He emerged only at the call of charity.

The meeting progressed smoothly, with its daily conferences. There the situation of each of the houses was discussed, and new superiors appointed. On several occasions, Benedict had asked to be relieved of his post. As we have already said, Santa Maria di Gesù, thanks to Benedict, had become a flourishing friary in which the reform had been solidly established. There was nothing to prevent a new Father Guardian taking over. The provincial superiors agreed.

However, Benedict was appointed Father Vicar to his successor. He was to give to the new Father Guardian the inestimable support of his experience and of the respect he had won in the eyes of the religious. This appointment was for three years. Benedict was then fifty-six years old.

During these three years, we find him following the same life of prayer, of penance, of work, as when he was Father Guardian; with this difference, however, that now freed from responsibility for the community, he could more easily devote himself to the love of God and neighbor.

He now withdrew more frequently to the mountain at the foot of which stood the friary. He had chosen a special place there. Under a tree which can still be seen and which has become enormous, he had arranged a kind of hermit's retreat. A little oratory has been built on the spot. We have climbed the slope which leads up to it. There is a splendid view from it stretching to the Bay of Palermo and to the summit of the mountain. The silence there is very impressive. Often, in this chosen spot, ecstasy would take complete possession of Benedict, rendering more and more intimate his union with God. Each day, love of the Lord became more and more demanding, and Benedict answered that demand by emptying himself more and more of self, in order to give greater and greater access to God.

All this was not done, however, without a struggle. We should find it very discouraging if the saints were exempt from the difficulties one meets in attempting to acquire virtue. But this is not so. We are encouraged to imitate the saints precisely by the courage and tenacity they have shown in overcoming their defects of nature and of temperament. So we are not displeased to learn that Benedict had a violent disposition which it sometimes took everything he had to control. In this connection, one occurrence is highly significant.

Not far from the friary there lived an insolent and gross young man who detested Benedict. Every time he met Benedict, he heaped insults on him, calling him a slave, a dog, a low wretch. Though he boiled inside at these insults, Benedict controlled himself, bent his head, pretended not to hear, and went on his way.

Exasperated by this calm behavior, the young man went beyond the limits of endurance by offering one of those insults which no Sicilian would take. Rage seized on Benedict, and he was just about to fling himself at the insulter, when the outraged countenance of Christ rose up before him. He immediately took hold of himself, but the effort to do so was so powerful that it brought on a copious nose-bleed.

In vivid contrast with this young man, however, were the petitioners who came each day in increasing numbers to the friary. What we say here about his charity applies also to his years as Father Guardian and right up to his death.

The first of the commandments is to love God with our whole heart, and with our whole mind, and with all our strength; and the second, which is similar to the first and inseparable from it, is to love our neighbor as ourselves. To neglect one commandment is to neglect the other; to observe the one necessarily entails the observance of the other. Benedict appreciated all this deeply. For him, it was not just a commandment; love was a necessity.

The influence he had acquired with God won for him the extraordinary power which he manifested all his life by the working of wonders. But we are convinced that it was still more his great love for his neighbor which led God to grant him everything he requested for his fellow-men.

He was no lofty wonder-worker who intervened in human affairs in a cold and remote fashion; he was a man full of gentleness, of goodness, of courtesy. All received the same welcome from him, and he never hid away however demanding the crowd might become. If there was any preference towards the petitioners, it was in favor of the humble and the lowly.

Once, his day ended with a long and exhausting interview with a rich woman, whom he consoled, enlightened, and encouraged. Afterwards, he said to the porter in passing that he was very tired. Then he went off to pray, which was his manner of seeking refreshment for body and soul. A few minutes later, an old woman, poor and miserable, and afflicted in many ways, arrived and asked to see "Fra Benedetto." Out of consideration for Benedict, the porter tried to put her off, saying that Benedict was sick and that she must come back some other time. But she insisted, with loud and vehement pleadings. The porter refused to budge. One can easily imagine the scene, full of eloquent gestures and whirling words.

Suddenly, Benedict made his appearance. His face filled with distress, he said to the astonished porter: "Why have you not called me to see this woman? No doubt, because she is poor and miserable? You have behaved badly! Charity should be shown equally towards all."

Thereupon, he led the poor woman to the parlor, and later sent her away consoled and encouraged, and with humble apologies for the manner in which she had been received. The porter had not recovered from his astonishment, puzzled how Benedict could have known that the woman was at the door, and still more astounded at the very humble apologies he had made to her.

We cannot recount here the innumerable miracles performed by Benedict, as reported in the processes of beatification and canonization. We shall therefore choose some of the most solidly established and most characteristic.

Four very pious women had come from Palermo to pass the day in a kind of retreat at the church of Santa Maria di Gesù. They were Eleanora, wife of Aurelio di Ferro, Eulalia Bemanuta, Lucrezia di Carlo, and Francesca di Beatrice. They had come in a coach, for the friary was some miles from Palermo by a very bad road.

At the end of the day, they set off for Palermo. Very soon, the coachman must have nodded off, for he let the reins hang slack on the mules. Irritated by the heat and by the flies, the mules took this as an open invitation to gallop along. At a turning not far from the friary, the coach overturned. The women were flung to the ground, and the frenzied animals began to draw the overturned coach along, trapping them. Their cries reached the people of the neighboring houses, who rushed out to help.

Eleanora lay on the ground clasping her five-month-old baby, killed in the accident. She was sobbing hysterically. By this time, the friars had come running from the house, Benedict among them. He asked the distressed mother why she was weeping so bitterly.

"Father," she answered, "I have lost my child, and I feel awful because I have come here and taken the child with me without my husband's permission."

"Have confidence in God," Benedict answered.

He took the baby into his arms, and reciting a prayer, he placed his hand on its forehead. Then he handed the baby back to its mother and told her to feed it.

"But what is the use, Father?" she protested. "The baby is dead."

And to convince Benedict, she put her finger into the Baby's still wide open mouth.

"Have faith, my daughter," he replied. "Just feed the baby."

As soon as she began to do so, the child gave all the signs of being vigorously alive.

Not content with this first miracle on this occasion, Benedict turned his attention to Lucrezia. She was pregnant at the time, and one of the wheels had run over her body. She too was wailing piteously, convinced that her child was dead. Benedict made the Sign of the Cross over her, reciting some favorite prayers. He assured her that when her time came, she would give birth to a healthy child. This prophecy came true. The beneficiaries of these prodigies and those who witnessed them, spread the fame of Benedict far and wide.

When Jesus met the widow, the woman whose only son was being carried to his grave, He could not resist the tears of the distressed woman, and He raised her son to life. It was the same sentiment that animated Benedict when he saw the anguish of these two women.

Nicholas Ferreri of Palermo and his wife Appolonia went one day into their garden, which bordered on that of Santa Maria di Gesù. With them were their two sons, Joseph aged fourteen years and his elder brother. We have already mentioned the violent temperament of the Sicilians, and here we have a dramatic example of it. There was a row between the two brothers, and the elder flung Joseph to the ground. Drunk with rage, he lifted a big stone and struck his brother repeatedly on the head with it. The boy vomited great quantities of blood and died in a few minutes.

On his way back to the friary, Benedict heard what had just occurred. He went into the garden, stood beside the corpse, and said to the parents:

"My children, have trust in God, and do not doubt His goodness."

Then, with a little saliva he made the Sign of the Cross on the dead boy's forehead, and walked away. He had scarcely taken ten paces when the dead boy opened his eyes, stirred, recovered his health, and immediately began to play as if nothing had happened.

Again, here is one of those miracles which reveals in Benedict the spirit of St. Francis. Water was short at the friary, and a charitable neighbor brought two barrels of it on his horse's back. Then he went off to the forest to gather wood which he used to sell to support his family.

The horse, loaded with wood, slipped and fell into a ravine when it was descending a mountain called Gibilrossa. Its master clambered quickly down, and found that the animal was dead. He was in despair, for that horse was the only means he had to support his family. He immediately thought of the charity of Fra Benedetto, and, running to the friary, he begged the Father Guardian to send Benedict back with him to the place of the accident. Moved with compassion, the Father Guardian did as he was requested. When Benedict reached the spot, he looked kindly at the poor man and said:

"Why, it's nothing. Help me to raise the horse."

Then he lifted up the horse's head, and immediately the horse, complete with its load, stood up, well and whole.

An entire book would not be enough to contain all the cases of the paralyzed who regained the use of their limbs, the blind to whom sight was restored, the pregnant women given help in difficult deliveries, those born infirm who were cured, and the mentally handicappy who received full use of their minds.

In certain cases, however, Benedict's intercession was not successful, no doubt because God judged it better that the patient should die rather than remain on earth. Whenever this was so, Benedict received interior light concerning it. To those who were petitioning him in such cases, the sick themselves or their relatives, he would then answer that they must unite themselves with the will of God, that they must be resigned, that they must let the Lord act as He knew to be best.

For those familiar with his usual way of answering, this was equivalent to a prediction of the immanent death of the patient for whom help had been sought, even when the doctors were saying that this sick person would certainly recover.

From all parts of Sicily, Italy, Spain, and Portugal, they came to see Benedict, bringing with them their sick and their maimed, and confiding to him their most desperate situations.

But even more than physical diseases, it was those of the soul which he sought to cure. Having received from God the gift of reading hearts, he revealed to poor sinners the extent of their misery, and then urged them to confess to a priest, assuring them that with God's pardon they would find peace again.

Hermit of St. Francis, then cook in a Franciscan friary, then Father Guardian of that friary, then its Father Vicar, such had been the changes in Benedict's life, and they were not yet ended. The superiors of the province would meet again in 1584, and once again they would express what for Benedict was the will of God.

8. HOW A SAINT DIES

His beloved solitude and peace had not been immediately restored to Benedict when he relinquished the office of Father
Guardian, since that of Father Vicar proved to be even more pre-
occupying for him. In the superior's absence, it was he who had
to assume responsibility for governing the house, in addition to
his constant and busy task of attending to its material matters.
The new provincial assembly, he hoped, would restore him to the
obscurity of his former condition, and his wish was granted. He
was freed from the burden of authority.

He returned to his kitchen. Such changes of status are quite
usual in the religious life, but are somewhat puzzling to men
hungry for the honors of authority and for its material advantages.
Where authority is regarded as no more than an onerous service,
it is to be expected that those who exercise it should be delivered
from its burden after a time. Thus, a man who was Father
Provincial will return to the ranks or to the fulfilment of a less
important post.

Far from regarding it as what we might call "a come down,"
Benedict joyfully accepted his return to the kitchen as a favor
granted to him by his superiors. However, very little had really
changed in his life since his first period as cook, and since that
time when he had spent Christmas Eve and Christmas morning in

ecstasy. Everywhere, people were talking about him as the Black Saint.

When he had to travel, he was obliged to do so by night, because otherwise he would be accompanied from village to village by a real escort of excited admirers, singing his praises and shouting "The Saint, the Saint!" This was sheer torture to Benedict.

One day, the Father Provincial, Father Serafino della Ficarra, had the idea, which he later indeed regretted, of arranging for Benedict to take part in a public ceremony. It was the feast of Corpus Christi, when the annual great procession would wind its way through the streets of Palermo. The members of the many religious houses of the city used to join in it.

Secretly vain of having a saint among his religious sons, the Father Provincial directed Benedict to carry the cross in front of the processional group of friars. Benedict immediately obeyed, and took his place at their head flanked by two acolytes.

Of course, what the imprudent provincial had not foreseen inevitably happened. Benedict went into ecstasy. He walked forward, his countenance radiant with light, his eyes fixed on Christ hanging on the Cross.

The excited rumor spread like wildfire through the streets that a miracle was about to occur. The crowd thronged around the Black Saint, everyone eager to see the wonder with his or her own eyes. People were knocked down and trampled in the hysterical crush.

The procession, which should have been marked by an atmosphere of calm and fervor, was now simply a wild tumult which the priests tried to control as best they could.

Father Serafino had learned his lesson. Never again would he direct Benedict to take part in a public ceremony.

All day long, the doorbell of Santa Maria rang, pulled by the innumerable visitors who came to see Benedict, to seek from him consolation and courage, to ask him to work a miracle, to obtain a cure for them from God. Rich and poor came to the friary, and were received in the same way, except that the poor received a greater measure of the courtesy and kindness shown to all.

The great ones of this world were among the petitioners. For instance, the viceroy of Sicily, Mark-Antony Colonna, who held Benedict in great affection and esteem. When his wife became gravely ill, he sent for Benedict. All the doctors' efforts had been to no avail. It only remained to have recourse to the Supreme Doctor, God Himself, and to the saint to whom he had delegated His power.

Benedict, sent by his Father Guardian, arrived at the viceroy's palace with one companion. There he was received with great respect and was taken immediately to the sick woman. She tried to kiss his hand, but, with what by now had become his instinctive reaction, he stuck his hands deeply into the ample sleeves of his habit.

The viceroy besought him to pray for her, that God might cure her. Smiling serenely, Benedict answered that there was no need for anxiety, since she would be quickly cured. Then, without further delay, he set off for Santa Maria di Gesù. Scarcely had he departed, when the sick woman suddenly felt well again.

We are not told whether Benedict was given another member of the community to help him in the kitchen. We must suppose that he had an assistant, for otherwise how could the cook for such a large community so frequently leave his work to see visitors? Unless, of course, he had some angels in permanent service!

Since Benedict's mortifications constantly increased, we may well wonder how he found the strength for his work, for his emotionally exhausting interviews in the parlor, for the nights spent in prayer before the tabernacle.

There, he would go into ecstasy. Such is the testimony given by Fra Michael di Girgenti during the process of beatification: "One night, I was sent by a friar to investigate how it was that, while Benedict was praying in the church, a radiance of splendor went out from him. I went there, and this is what I distinctly saw. The lights in the choir were out, and yet that whole area was bathed in light. We could find no explanation for this, other than that it was a celestial radiance."

But Benedict's strength was visibly diminishing. Only through superhuman courage was he succeeding in staying on his feet, always affable and smiling, always ready to do a service.

Five years had passed since his return to the kitchen, and Benedict was now sixty-three years old. His whole life had been one of humble service; never had he been a burden to others in the least way. His death had the same quality of selflessness and humility, occasioning for his brethren neither fatigue nor undue demands on their services.

In February 1589, Benedict became so gravely ill that he seemed to be on the point of death. John Dominic Rubiano, a very rich merchant of Palermo and an ardent admirer of Benedict, had expressed to the Father Guardian a deep desire to be present at Benedict's death. Word was therefore sent to him, and he came immediately.

He talked to Benedict about God, about his soul, and said how saddened he was at the thought of losing him so soon. Benedict calmly replied:

"This time, it is God's will that I should recover from my disease. It will not be so the next time; but I am ready, for my life is finished."

Rubiano, who knew how great was Benedict's prophetic gift, returned home, reassured that the saint would recover. But that recovery was short-lived. On March 4th, he fell sick again, devoured by an intense and persistent fever. His brethren, remembering the prediction he had made to Rubiano, knew then that Benedict's last days had begun. There was desolation among the members of the community, since each of them looked upon him as his guide and spiritual master. All tried to comfort him in his infirmities, and to diminish his sufferings in every way possible.

God had informed Benedict about the exact day and hour of his death, as well as about the most minute circumstances accompanying it. Father Ambrose di Palizzi, a superior of the order with a deep affection for Benedict, remained at his bedside. With the simplicity which characterizes the attitude of the servants of God towards death, Father Ambrose said to him:

"We shall have our work cut out for us on the day you die, Benedict. Just think of the throng of people who will come here!"

Benedict answered calmly:

"Oh, set your mind at rest about that, Father. There will be scarcely anyone here on the day I die, and that will be a very good thing. But unless you bury me immediately, such a huge crowd will come that you will really have a very difficult time. That is why I specially ask you to bury me immediately after my death."

We shall see later how that prophecy was fulfilled.

Benedict's illness lasted exactly one month. During that time, no one heard the least complaint from him, despite his great suffering; nor did he ever ask for anything which could have relieved his suffering.

Those who tended him during this month testified that he prayed constantly, either vocally or absorbed in interior contemplation. One day, someone asked him if he was thirsty. "Yes," he answered, "but I must put up with it patiently, since our Lord too was thirsty on the Cross."

The doctors prescribed medicines and treatments of all kinds. He accepted them, in a spirit of simple obedience, but was content to remark with a smile:

"Why all the attention to this poor body, and what good are these medicines? Our Lord accepted great anguish and sufferings during His Passion, so why should I not endure what I have to suffer?"

Twenty-nine days had passed since Benedict had to take to his bed. He knew that he was on the eve of his death, and so he asked to receive the sacraments.

According to custom, all the friars gathered around Benedict at this time. Before receiving Holy Viaticum, he turned to the community, and in a very clear voice he asked his brethren, present and absent, to forgive him whatever scandal he might have caused them. The greatest of sinners could not have spoken with deeper sincerity. Then, he recollected himself and, his face radiant with his ardent faith, he received the Viaticum and then the anointing.

One of his brethren, thinking the time of death had come, stepped forward with a lighted blessed candle. Benedict said to him:

"My son, my hour has not yet come. Put out the candle. When the moment does come, I shall tell you."

Benedict and his brethren spent that whole night in prayer. The moment of his death was approaching. Watching, they saw his face transformed, his eyes fixed on heaven. Then, suddenly, he turned to them and said:

"Place chairs here for those holy women who have come to visit me; but how can you find room for all the virgins who are with them?"

The religious told him that they could see no one, but he answered:

"Indeed! Do you not see St. Ursula with the company of her virgins?"

The brethren at first thought he was delirious, but nothing of the kind! His mind had already gone forward into the supernatural world which was awaiting him, and he could see visions beyond the power of human eyes. Right up to the end, he preserved both complete clarity of mind and absolute serenity. His union with God was complete, and it kindled his countenance with celestial radiance. According to the formal testimony of those who witnessed his death, a wonderful perfume filled the room, a palpable realization of one of St. Paul's exhortations: "Be the good odor of Christ."

The hour of his death was now at hand. Gathering all his strength, he painfully raised himself to a sitting position, and said to Friar William:

My brother, my time has now come. You can light the candles."

He crossed his hands on his breast, and pronounced the names of Jesus, Mary, and Francis. Then, lying down again, he spoke the words of Jesus on the Cross: "Into your hands, O Lord, I commend my spirit," and gently and serenely he died. It was seven o'clock on the evening of the 4th of April, 1589, Easter Tuesday. Benedict was 63 years old. He had joined the Hermits of St. Francis at the age of 21, had remained with them for 15 years, and had spent the final 27 years of his life in the Order of Friars Minor.

9. THE FIRST CANONIZED BLACK AFRICAN

In hot countries, it is customary to bury the dead very soon after death. One can readily appreciate the reason for this. As soon, therefore, as his brethren had mastered their sorrow, they began to prepare Benedict for burial, having first taken away everything they could keep as relics. The body was then removed to the community church where the friars chanted the Office for the Dead. Immediately afterwards, the remains were laid to rest in their tomb in the cemetery of the religious, close by the church. By this time, night had fallen.

The fear of rapid decomposition was not the sole motive for haste in Benedict's burial. Everyone remembered his prediction. To leave the body of a saint, such as he, exposed to the tumultuous and rash veneration of a crowd, over-excited by devotion, would have been to risk the worst disorders. The body would have been torn to pieces by a frenzied crowd seeking relics. The only people at the funeral, therefore, were the friars, Benedict's merchant friend Rubiano, the doctor, and the Most Reverend Louis Torres, archbishop of Monreale, later cardinal.

Next day the news reached Palermo with the effect of an earth tremor. The chroniclers tell us that the road to the friary was soon so swarming with people that it was almost impossible to move. All ranks of society, priests and laity, men and women, rich and poor, were present in the crush. All these pilgrims wanted to see him whom they were now calling St. Benedict, to touch him, to obtain some miracle. All hoped to obtain some relic which would prolong in their home the miraculous influence of the Black Saint.

A great shock awaited them when they discovered that he had already been placed in the tomb. The viceroy of Sicily, informed by a note from the Father Guardian, galloped to the friary in his carriage and only with difficulty secured passage through the swarming crowd. He insisted so vehemently on seeing once again his friend's face, that the Father Guardian had to yield. The tomb was opened. Three times an attempt was made to lower a lighted candle into the tomb, but each time it was extinguished. The viceroy had to resign himself to not getting his wish.

The crowd received, however, an extraordinary consolation. A perfume of great sweetness permeated the church and the whole friary. This had the effect of increasing still more everyone's desire to take away some relic. The friars had to cut up the clothes Benedict had worn, including his religious habit, and to distribute tiny pieces to the crowd. The community came near to being stripped of every relic of Benedict they possessed.

During the following four months, the chroniclers tell us, the friary church never emptied. Besides the people of Palermo itself, people came from all over Sicily, and pilgrimages were organized from Italy, Spain, and Portugal.

After his death, but with greater abundance, Benedict continued the prodigies which he had so often performed during his life for the relief of human suffering. Many were miraculously cured, many raised from the dead.

Let one account suffice as typical. It is one of the miracles accepted during the process of canonization, and it is contained in the bull by which Pope Pius VII placed Benedict among the saints.

It has to do with a nine-year-old boy, a native of Benedict's own

San Filadelfo. His name was Francis Centinius. He had been accidentally injured by a blow on the throat by a ball, and the artery was so damaged that he was on the point of death. A relic of Benedict was placed on the wound. The boy was immediately cured, and there was no trace of scar or injury.

Because of the evidence of widespread veneration, the ecclesiastical authorities gave permission for the body to be exhumed and put in a place of greater honor. This was done on the 7th of May, 1592, three years after the saint's death. The body was found intact and emitting the same perfume which had filled the church and the friary at the time of his death.

Among the eminent people present at the exhumation was the learned Dominican, Father Magis, who had been one of Benedict's great friends and who had often come to consult him about the difficulties he encountered in his theological studies. The presence of this erudite religious of an order other than that of St. Francis, shows how great had been the influence of Benedict during his lifetime.

Father Magis was stunned at seeing Benedict's body intact after three years, and at the perfume it exuded. He tenderly kissed the feet of his friend. Benedict's body was placed in a precious casket and lifted to a raised niche in the sacristy of the church.

This proved to be an act of imprudence whose dire consequences were soon realized. From that moment, there was a ceaseless influx of pilgrims into the sacristy. At certain times, the crowd was so great that many had a long wait before being able to take their place before the body of the saint, to pray there, and to ask from him the miracles which he worked with such generosity. Disputes sometimes arose, those who were already in the sacristy refusing to give place to others who were waiting to enter.

The friars, and particularly the sacristan, were upset at no longer being able to use the sacristy freely; while the pilgrims were most disgruntled when they were refused access to the sacristy at the time that priests and ministers were vesting for the sacred ceremonies.

Requests came from all quarters that the body should be transferred into the church. The Holy See authorized this, but stipulated that the transfer must take place without any manifestation of cult, the process of beatification being still pending.

This transference took place on the 3rd of October, 1611, in the presence of the cardinal archbishop of Palermo. Benedict's body was placed in a glass casket so that all could see it, and the casket was set up to the left of the altar of the Blessed Virgin. This event gave greater impetus to the fervor of the crowd, who ceaselessly came to pray to the saint and to ask for new miracles. Those whose prayers had been heard placed before the glass casket huge wax candles, banners or pictures on which they had painted the scene of their cure, and even silver or plaster casts of the diseased limbs that had been healed.

The Church did not remain indifferent to the extraordinary occurrences which followed the death of Benedict. In such cases, the Church has a duty to intervene, either to denounce a superstition or to authenticate what is taking place. It is then that the process of beatification is inaugurated to be followed by that of canonization. These processes are carried out with the utmost rigor. Eyewitnesses are called and must testify on oath to what they have seen. These witnesses are themselves subjected to invstigation to establish that they are thoroughly reliable.

On the 5th of August, 1594, the first session of this process opened at the palace of the archbishop of Palermo; and in the course of it ninety-seven eyewitnesses were heard. The second ordinary process took place at Palermo in 1622. The records of both were sent to the Sacred Congregation of Rites.

These processes are long and expensive, since they entail the intervention of many collaborators, experts, judges, copyists. The Franciscan Order in Sicily was poor, and could not pay out the very considerable sum needed for the continuation of the process. The latter remained in abeyance, therefore, but this could not be said about the popular devotion towards the Black Saint. Finally, on the 31st of July, 1743, Pope Benedict XIV beatified Benedict the Black.

The next and final step would be the proclamation of his holiness to the entire Catholic Church. This would be the work of the process of canonization. Begun on the 3rd of July, 1780, it ended with the proclamation by Pope Pius VII on the 25th of May, 1807, that the Blessed Benedict had been judged worthy of being raised to the altars of the Church, and was therefore to be known henceforth as St. Benedict. He was the first African of the black race thus solemnly canonized by the Church.

In the manner of the saints, Benedict had exacted revenge for the crime committed by the Whites against his people and his race whom they had reduced to slavery. He had lavished good upon them, easing their sufferings, curing their diseases, even restoring to despairing parents their child who had died. In him, God fulfilled the wonderful promise of the beatitudes.

He who would normally have been looked down upon by the learned, found them coming to him, an ignorant and illiterate man, to seek the benefit of his infused knowledge in resolving their intellectual difficulties. The great ones of the earth, among them the viceroy of Sicily, would come to him for advice in their difficulties. The sons of those who had reduced his family to slavery, pleaded with him to become their leader and their guide.

The body of the Black Saint rests in the little Church of Santa Maria di Gesù in Palermo. A wax mask awkwardly attempts to restore his features, but certainly distorts them since they are not those of an African. The poor desiccated fingers are raised in a gesture of blessing outside a silken tunic which is also in its own way a travesty. The people of Palermo have forgotten the road to Santa Maria di Gesù; at least they never take it in order to venerate the remains of St. Benedict. It is his Black brothers, we are convinced, who will rediscover that way.